ISBN 978-1-330-85603-1
PIBN 10114410

English
Français
Deutsche
Italiano
Español
Português

www.forgottenbooks.com

Mythology Photography **Fiction**
Fishing Christianity **Art** Cooking
Essays Buddhism Freemasonry
Medicine **Biology** Music **Ancient**
Egypt Evolution Carpentry Physics
Dance Geology **Mathematics** Fitness
Shakespeare **Folklore** Yoga Marketing
Confidence Immortality Biographies
Poetry **Psychology** Witchcraft
Electronics Chemistry History **Law**
Accounting **Philosophy** Anthropology
Alchemy Drama Quantum Mechanics
Atheism Sexual Health **Ancient History**
Entrepreneurship Languages Sport
Paleontology Needlework Islam
Metaphysics Investment Archaeology
Parenting Statistics Criminology
Motivational

PINEY WOODS

AND

ITS STORY

By
LAURENCE C. JONES
Principal of the Piney Woods Country Life School.

With an Introduction by
S. S. McCLURE

NEW YORK   CHICAGO

Fleming H. Revell Company

LONDON   AND   EDINBURGH

New York: 158 Fifth Avenue
Chicago: 17 North Wabash Ave
London: 21 Paternoster Square
Edinburgh: 75 Princes Street

To my Wife and Mother who, from the first day they knew me, have given their best for me, this book is affectionately dedicated.

INTRODUCTION

THIS is the story, told by himself, of a Negro of education, intelligence and sensitiveness, who turned his back upon everything that usually makes life worth living for people of his kind and went, without money or influence, or even an invitation, among the poorest and most ignorant of his race, for the sole purpose of helping them in every way within his power.

He has told it persuasively and sincerely. It is a valuable human document; a paragraph in a vital chapter of American history. I was glad to publish in *McClure's Magazine* the first record of his inspiring work. It is difficult to believe that there is any good citizen in this country, white or black, of whatever shade of belief in regard to the larger aspects of the " Negro question," who will not be glad to join with me in wishing God-speed to its author and the remarkable school he has built.

S. S. McClure.

New York.

FOREWORD

IT was during the lingering dusk of a never-to-be-forgotten evening, and the twilight imparted a perfect serenity. In the west the sun had left in its trail a shimmer of red and gold, and only the evening hymns of birds obtruded on the silence. Finally Mrs. Harris, the dear wife of our constant friend, Dr. D. J. Harris, resumed the conversation and spoke of the increasing faith which her husband had in the work at Piney Woods and of the ultimate benefit that he felt would accrue from it for those for whom it was maintained; and she also remarked the interest with which he had read and re-read my little story, "Up Through Difficulties." Then, departing for the moment from her reminiscent mood, she said, speaking for herself: "It is a story, Mr. Jones, everyone should know. Piney Woods and its history has taken itself out of the realm of mere friendly individual claim and praise, and now belongs to the public. You not only owe it to the public, but to yourself as well, to gather and compile the sketches which from time to time you have written, and, blending them with 'Up Through Difficulties,' to issue the whole in form for the many rather than the few."

Last summer also, during my speaking tour on the Redpath Chautauqua Circuit, after each lecture I was asked by many people if I had published anything relative to my work in book form. And so, there you are, dear reader, and I trust, good friend. But I beg you not to think of this little book as the story of my life. It is much more than that; it is the story of that which to me is more than my life. It is the story of the lighting of a torch—a torch indeed, but one *blazing like the sun,* one which shall furnish a new and compelling inspiration to the children of many generations, each striving to perform his or her part in making brighter the home, the race, the community, the nation, and the world.

And should not I, " Piney Woods " Jones, acknowledge my appreciation of the time and thought which my teacher, Miss Mary Grove Chawner, of college days and since, has given to the work? Should I not also remember with deep thankfulness Mr. Harvey Ingham, Mr. J. E. Reizenstein, Mr. Frank Hartman, Mr. A. A. Moore, Mr. F. A. Moscrip, Mr. Fred. Lazell, and Mr. J. L. Waite, who with their trenchant pens have stood loyally behind the school from the beginning? I must also thank Miss Alice French, Rev. Benjamin Brawley, Mrs. Mary Ovington White, and Col. Robert T. Kerlin for their kindness in reading the manuscript. For the effort of these friends, and for the kindness of all the others who are mentioned in these pages, who can tell my gratitude? From the bottom of my heart I thank them; I thank them all to-day.

LAURENCE C. JONES.

BRAXTON, MISS.

Contents

ILLUSTRATIONS

I

MY OWN BEGINNINGS

WOODED hills, a shimmering river, and rugged cedar bluffs give St. Joseph a picturesque setting; mills and locomotives and steamboats keep it busy with travel and trade; while magnificent churches and schools, hotels and parks, give it civic pride and make it what it is—a pretty city, the busiest and richest of its size in the state of Missouri.

Here I was born and raised; and as I think now of the many notable features of the town, if I were asked to name the single one that in point of beauty or interest surpasses all others, my reply would be hesitant and doubtful, but in the days when I was a little boy I should have answered promptly and even with a challenge: "The Pacific Hotel of course."

The "Pacific" was not only one of the most popular hotels in the West; from front to rear, from cellar floor to the top of the tallest chimney, it was everything that makes a hotel equal to the demands of wealth and culture. Every good and

15

perfect pleasure seemed crowded within its walls—music and bloom and color, warmth when the days were cold, coolness when the days were hot, luxury and life and beauty in every form. But what above all else made the Pacific such a joy to my childish heart was the fact that it belonged to my father. Truth! Was he not the porter there? It was his hotel and I, a frequent visitor, made much of by those about, was one small lad who surveyed vast possessions.

Everybody had a word for "John." It was "Well, John, I'm back again"—a handshake, a slap on the shoulder, and my father's big laugh booming out. "No, no, John, just keep the change." "Well, by all that's good and bad, John, are you here yet? Can't they get rid of you at all? Ha! ha! ha!" "Well, good-bye, John, be good to yourself." "Hello, John." "Howdy do, John." "Oh, John." "Oh, Jo—ohn!" There were all sorts of voices, inflections, and accents, with laughs, growls, jokes, requests, and orders.

All tones fell lightly upon my ear. Then, almost without fail, I would hear one of the voices, a heavy, rumbling, bass one, say, "Your boy, John?" as a white hand descended upon my head. "Want to get rid of him, give him away, hire him out or something? Better let me take him along;

I need a boy just like that." There was always somebody claiming to want me and trying to make a bargain with my Dad for possession; and it took me a long time to learn that they were only joking. One day when a big man was gravely making arrangements for me to go North and be a lumberjack, I answered the usual question as to how that would suit me by rudely piping, "Rats!" and the deal came to a sudden stop. Then, while my would-be employer went on his way, his broad shoulders shaking with amusement, I myself sat aghast, my little world in ruins. From my father, however, came the word of speedy retribution: "Son, you drivin' mos' too big a team to-day. Show-off is a bad boss. Can't have him 'roun' this hotel a-tall—nope, not a-tall. Run along home, son, an' tell your mother 'bout it."

My father, plain, strict, and practical, was a valorous, verbal supporter of the rod. I can hear him now, placidly advising my mother, " Put the bud to him; jus' tan his jacket." Yet he himself was never known to put his preaching into practice. My mother, however, theoretically opposed to such doctrine, could somehow get her hands on a long, keen switch, peel the leaves off it, and apply it as it was most needed, more quickly than anybody else I knew.

One great and special treat of those days was to accompany my father when he went to "make" the trains and watch him "git the business," as he termed it. His, it seemed to me, was a captivating way of raising his hand to his cap, with a deferential yet crisp half-query, half-statement, "Hotel? Pacific Hotel," as the passengers came down the steps. Next his erect figure moved away, a grip in each of his hands, while I, trying to walk just like him, strode alongside, looking forward to the time when I, too, should be a man—and a porter.

Yes, I would be a porter, and I would have a stubby pipe and lots of fat cigars, which the drummers and other big men would give me; and on my Sunday afternoons off I would sit by the fire, or, in warm weather, on the little front porch at home, and smoke, and smoke, and smoke. My eyes would look gladder and kinder than ever while I blew rings and watched them curl and fade away, and the way I'd puff would be a wonder. Yet long before, I had almost proved myself a prodigy by appearing on a program and declaiming:

> "I'll never use tobacco, no!
>   It is a filthy weed;
>   I'll never put it in my mouth,
>   Said little Robert Reed."

One day, as I was sunning outside the building, at peace, so far as I knew, with all the world, a storm-cloud, in the person of Egg-eye, one of the neighborhood's little terrors, rose on the horizon and blew briskly down the walk in my direction. So far all right. His face was very innocent and his eyes fixed straight ahead, and this was all right also. Just as he came abreast of me, however, his feet gave a funny little shuffle; his shoulder, the one nearest me, hunched up; and his elbow flew out like a rigid wing and disturbed his progress by jabbing against me. Indignant, surprised, he wheeled about and halted. "Oh, it's Mister Jones," he crowed; "come pretty near knocking me down. Better run over me next time and be done with it." He jerked his hat more to one side, rolled his eyes around to make sure there were no onlookers, drew nearer and belligerently lowered his voice: "Think you own dis here hotel, don't you? Think yo' pa owns it. Well, you git that out o' yo' fool head or I'll knock it out. And you"—his scornful eye scanned my white blouse and tight little velvet trousers—"stylish, ain't you? Got on yo' Sunday clothes! Huh! don't you cheep. Don't you call me liar."

Egg-eye knew I had not tried to cheep. Around the hotel, however, I was bound to be on my best behavior. To be involved in a noisy quarrel or fight would have been disastrous to me; moreover, Egg-eye was much larger than I. Down in my heart raged the desire to call him several choice names that I knew of and had not yet dared to utter—names that would have annihilated him at once. My father was somewhere about, however, and might hear me; so I backed away gradually, gradually, hoping to get near enough to the door before the enemy suspected to get inside with some degree of dignity. It seemed that I should never reach that door. Meanwhile Egg-eye had thrust forward his jaw and gone through with all the preliminaries, and the next thing would have been the actual attack. But the blows were never dealt; the enemy saw someone approaching and vanished.

When my father heard my version of the affair he seemed to enjoy it immensely. After a while, however, he said reflectively, "So that's the big question, is it? Do I own this hotel? Well, son, I own my part of it an' you can always count on your ol' Dad ownin' his part of anything good that's round about him." Having thus restored my happiness he added to it by giving me a penny and a nickel—the penny, according to established custom, to be spent for candy or chewing gum, while

The Old Cabin
Made into a School Building

the nickel was to go into the iron pig on the shelf at home to be used at some distant day when I might be starting out for college, or when I might want to be an expressman and buy a big span of Missouri mules.

To my father anything out of the ordinary was "big." There were "big guns," "big colonels," and even "big drummers." But what most quickly claimed my interest was to hear my father say that it was going to be a "big day" down town and remark to my mother that she had better get the boy ready rather early so that he might reach the hotel before the streets were too crowded.

Perhaps the occasion would be a circus, and of course the parade would pass the "Pacific"—they all did; or it might be a political demonstration of some sort. In course of time I had come to be a vociferous supporter of many movements and platforms. One among the spectators crowding the windows and balconies of the hotel, I would wave a flag or banner and shrilly cheer, rooting for something or somebody just as suited whoever had charge of me at the moment. Not all the glitter of bright-hued trappings, of elephants and Shetland ponies, of monkeys and clowns, thrilled me as did austere columns of men marching along, timed by the splendid blare of brass horns and of the mutter of drums and the squealing of fifes. I loved it all—almost too intensely, it seemed, for there was something about it that overwhelmed and vaguely hurt me, and that to the heart of childhood was a great and infinite mystery.

As for Old Glory, as my father always called a large flag, I can never see it lift its colors on the breeze without poignantly recalling one day—the awesome day on which for the first time I saw my father cry, the first time I ever saw him " break plumb down and make a fool of himself "—that being his way of speaking of the occasion the one time that I heard him mention it.

He and I were on our way downtown one morning—I do not remember what the day was, whether it was Washington's or Lincoln's birthday or what —but anyway on the front of a building abutting upon the walk before us a large flag hung drooping and inert in the chill morning mist. The papers the night before had told of a most revolting instance of mob violence, and as my father spoke of it at breakfast his face looked hard and set, and the steady, steely look in his eyes somehow made him seem almost a stranger. I wondered if that was the way he used to look when he was a soldier—" United States Army, ol' Company K, '67 to '76, hon'able discharge." He had spoken to me but once since we left the house, and then in a dull heavy voice that was as unfamiliar as the expression on his face. Childlike I felt its mood and was in its shadow, and that short trip might have been remembered even without further distinction; but terror stalked that morning—tragedy was abroad.

We came abreast of the flag-decked front, and just then obeying a caprice of the wind the banner lifted in the grand way it has and streamed out just above us, its silken breadth spreading out with a rush and rustle that would have lured me, momentarily at least, from my woe, only as it reached its greatest expanse it seemed to fling from its folds a terrible cry. Stentorian, wild, sad, defiant, the sound seemed to fill all the air and to die away in a tremolo that left the soul full of chill and shudders. That cry, I somehow realized to my heart-sickening, paralyzing terror, had been uttered by my father—by my father! Why?

Ur-r-r-r-ee-woo-oo-aoo! The awful sound again! My father had come to an abrupt standstill, his eyes gazing unseeingly upon the banner and far beyond it as though he were addressing in that queer language some invisible and distant throng. " Oo hoo-oo! Stan' by Ol' Glory! No difference if dey lynches a black man every day for forty years! We kin stand it—us black folks—we kin

stand it agin de day of reckonin'!" In his excitement my Dad had gone back to the native manner
of speech which he so carefully tried to avoid in
calmer moments. "Cl' Glory's still a-wavin'!
Reckon she's gwine a be de shelter and de kiverin
for a cussed thing like that fo'ever? No, no! by
——!" His clenched fist struck my shoulder a
blow that spun me around and I should have fallen
had it not been for the support of the wall. A
harsh, heavy sob choked his utterance, and watch-
ing him, my own face wet with the copious tears
of childish excitement and sympathy, I saw big
tears roll down his cheeks. By the time we reached
the hotel, however, the sun had come out, my Dad
was himself again, and all was well.

As I grew older I learned more and more to
appreciate my father's homely wisdom, his droll
sayings, and his sturdy way of facing life. He
seemed to take things as they came, but whenever
it was in his power to do so he saw to it that they
came his way. He was ambitious for me, but
sometimes expressed himself in such a manner that
one not knowing him might have thought he had
queer ideas as to an occupation for me. About my
childhood's savings bank, for instance, he always
said that the money in it was to help me start to
college or to help me buy a span of mules. What

he really meant was that if I should happen to fail to get to college I should be prepared to do something else to make myself useful. It might even develop that I should have to be a drayman as he was when he first started out for himself; and if that happened he at least wanted me to have a good team and not have to begin with a pair of goats as he did. I should in any case be that much ahead of the old generation.

It was very interesting to hear him talk of his youthful days down in Alabama, also of his life in the army; and it seemed almost wonderful, how through so many hardships and temptations he developed the personality that made him a general favorite, the ability that made him a great reader, and the character that earned for him the title "Honest John."

As for his attainments in life, he seemed to feel that in being able to hold down the job at the hotel as he did, he had traveled far and achieved much. Holding the idea that he was "cut out" for a porter, he considered himself fortunate in having found his niche. No doubt there were higher positions, but he did not covet them. "To be the right man in the right place," he would say, "was a good enough job for anybody." Such was the spirit in which for all those years he did his work, and every now and then, coming across some old book of my boyhood, I am as proud of the import of the mis-spelled inscription scrawled on the fly-leaf as I was when I first wrote it:

" Laurence Jones, Sun of Onest John Jones use to be a solger, Potah at ' Pacific' Hotel. Old Com-puny K 'Onnabel dischage. St. josef Mussura."

Such easy-going philosophy as my father's had little place in my mother's conception of life, either as it was then or as it was to be in the years ahead. That one should be supinely content in whatever place he chanced to fall was something that she simply could not understand. In her creed, un-consciously and unfalteringly held, to do well ac-cording to one's strength was not ambition but a plain, unvarnished duty. It was what we were here for—to do the very best we could, and only in that way could we show our appreciation of life and its possibilities. This creed was not only a part of her belief, but its golden thread was woven and interwoven in her nature; so that aside from the sweetness of her personality, there was a strength, an irresistible something about her, that made her very presence a power for good. In her heart a light was ever glowing, diffusing radiance, courage, and enthusiasm upon all around. No towering pine in her native Wisconsin forests ever pointed upward more naturally than did she in her ideals of life.

A fragile little woman my mother was, all temperament and dreams—in reality an idealist, yet possessing that intense practical industry so often demonstrated by the women of her race, who dream most splendid dreams and bravely strive, through the humble mediums within their reach, to make their dreams come true. To such a one the washtub and ironing-board, the cook-stove, the needle, and the scrubbing-brush, are all but homely tools to be most diligently used. The average unskilled colored man, hardworking and steady though he be, earns hardly more than enough to provide for his family a meagre livelihood, and further than that his earnings can not reach. The simple luxuries, the daintier necessities and comforts, the little touches of beauty here and there, must come from another hand. Some one else provides the pretty walls and hangings, the new dress for a special occasion, perhaps even a piano or a porch or an additional room on the house; some one else may even send the son or daughter away to college. And who has not seen it—the colored woman at her work, infusing faith into her drudgery, toiling day after day, year after year, while slowly but surely her surroundings begin to assume the color of her dreams?

Such a home-maker was my mother; and yet her work was such that she was away from home much of the time. She was an excellent seamstress and often went out to sew by the day, and she also served sometimes at ladies' clubs in the evening. Meanwhile we children—my sister and myself—often found ourselves and the house in the care of "Aunt" 'Liza, an aged woman of the neighborhood who made her living by helping out in different homes, and who, as my mother and everybody else said, was as good an old soul as ever lived.

Aunt 'Liza was a noted character in the church to which she belonged, a class-meeting priestess of unique distinction. She had a great store of maxims—"Bible-teachings," she called them, "good for the healing of the soul," and these she drew upon as time and occasion demanded. "Thou shellt not steal," she said, "neither sugar, ner jelly, ner nothin' else;" "Thou shellt not tell lies an' b'ar false witness agins' thy neighbor, little sister ner brother ner nobody;" "When somebody fetch you a clip on one o' yo' cheeks, turn de ether one, an' ef he fetch you a clip on dat one, den de Lawd be wid de righteous;" "Honor yo' pappy and yo' mammy, an' don't be sassin an' talkin' back,

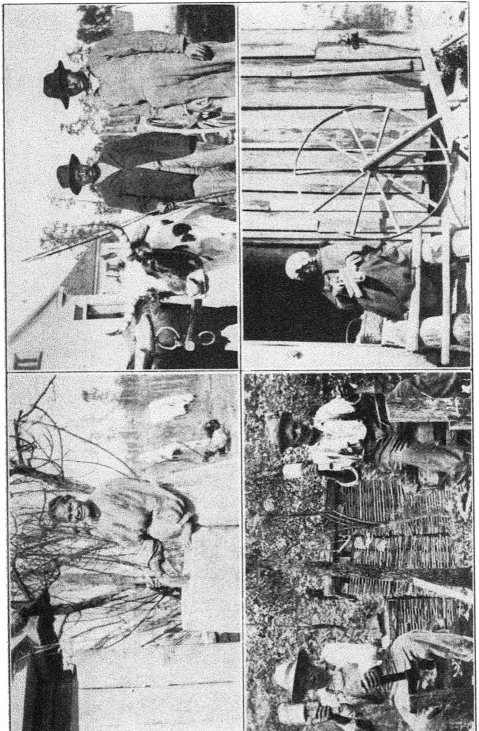

kase chillun should be seed an' not hyeard." There were many others of these garbled sayings, but the one most often used was: " Chillun should be seed an' not hyeard."

Sometimes late in the night I would awake and hear Aunt 'Liza " agonizin' in pra'er," tearfully beseeching blessings and forgiveness of sins, for herself, her church, her friends and neighbors, and the whole, round world. Sometimes she would be singing softly, reflectively, rocking back and forth in her low chair beside the fire—not a rocking-chair but a straight-back, splint-bottomed chair that she always brought in from the kitchen. The room would be dim, for even when she was knitting she wanted the lights low when it was late. If the night was wild or dreary the hymn never failed to end in tremulous query—mournful, haunting, weird beyond description:

> An-nd am I a-borned to-oo die,
> To-oo a-la-ay this a-body down?

On another night without prelude or warning the song would ring out rapturously:

> Jes look a-yander a-what I see—
> Hise de window, let de dove come in;
> A ban' of angels a-comin' for me—
> Oh! hise de window, let de dove come in.

When the song was over, however, I was likely

to hear something like this: " Laurence, honey, is you wake? You's young chil' an' souple in de jints; wisht you'd git up an' fetch my pieces an' things; I been off a-jubilatin' in my soul an' dat ornery cat done ketched my basket—quilt pieces, knittin' an' all, an' tuck 'em way back under de bed."

My mother always demanded a full report of our behavior during her absence, and if we had been good there were rewards ensuing, the greatest being one of the wonderful stories that my mother herself would tell in her wonderful way. Who could ever forget such hours as those when I with my sisters listened to those gripping tales? Sometimes we were on a bench in the kitchen; on summer evenings out on the little front porch in the moonlight; but best of all were the winter evenings in the front room by the fire.

As I was the only boy in the family, all the hopes and ambitions that the maternal heart cherishes were centered upon me. I was expected to possess all the commendable traits of my ancestors. Also it seemed to be expected that I should emulate all the men of my race who had come into prominence since the founding of America. Meanwhile, to all else, it was understood that I should add something of my own individuality. In the family it was fondly hoped that I might be " cut out" for a lawyer, a doctor, an editor, a minister, a " big" business man, a professor; I might get into Congress; and—what seemed to my childish mind most impossible of all—I had to be a gentleman. Last, but not least among the responsibilities awaiting me when I grew up, I was to be a man— the one decision that had my own fervent approval. In this I should be like my father, so often admiringly described as a " man;" and also like my mother's kinsmen, of whom she often talked—all " men."

On one of these kinsmen, strange prophecy of the future, my mind somehow lingers to-day. My great-grandfather was born in Virginia, but while yet a young man purchased his freedom and removed to Pennsylvania. There Robert Foster, my mother's father, was born. This grandfather of mine, I have learned, was wholly or largely responsible for the founding of an educational institution in Michigan in 1848. At that time colored people were not admitted to the public schools of Ohio; and Robert Foster and some of his brothers and friends decided to establish a school for their children, which they did after going to Michigan. The institution thus founded was open to all " regardless of color, sex, or religious affiliation," and was incorporated under the laws of the state of Michigan as a manual labor institute. So far as we have been able to learn, this was the first school to be established in this country for industrial training of colored boys and girls.

Once a year Foster would go east to solicit funds and make friends for the race. So on my frequent pilgrimages upon a similar mission I have to remember that, after all, I have come by my inheritance justly; I am simply "taking after" my grandfather.

II

SCHOOLDAYS

I WELL remember my first day at school. First my mother kissed me and said good-bye, and after I got to the building Miss Sadie gave me a seat, and then everything seemed to grow dim and lonely. Within a few minutes a big tear rolled down my burning cheek; others followed, and still more when I looked around to find everybody gazing at me. Miss Sadie called me to her desk and asked what was the matter, and between sobs I told her that I was tired, sleepy, and hungry, and that my mother needed me at home. She said that any little boy with all those things the matter with him surely ought to be excused for a little while. So my mother had been home only a few minutes when she saw me coming into the yard astride the shoulders of a larger boy who had volunteered to carry me back.

After the first day, however, the schoolroom became more attractive, and within the next few years I passed through the different grades of the grammar department. My first outside work was that of shining shoes; somewhat later I helped the porter shine shoes in Billy Rhodes' barber shop, the largest in the town at the time. Then in one memorable autumn I entered the high school. Here I found that I was not very enthusiastic about Latin and similar studies. I had found that the more boots I blacked the better I could get along, and I wanted something that would be a help in the future.

Another thing that made me want a more practical education was a famous old book that had been sent to me from Rock Island by my Aunt Sally. This was " Robinson Crusoe," the first book, after the Bible, that made any deep impression upon me. I read it on an average of once a month, and spent my spare time trying to find another book just like it. The story of the free, untrammeled life of the hero, making his own civilization, overcoming physical obstacles by his resourcefulness and building and making things with his hands to meet his needs, impressed me greatly. In comparison with such a life the things that I was studying in the high school seemed vain and futile, and by the close of my first half-year my work in the St. Joseph High School had become unendurable.

I have no doubt that this book and the constructive stories told in the Bible led my mind and hands into constructive play when not at work. I had the best backyard garden in the neighborhood, and our chickens always looked the best and produced the most eggs. I also kept the loft of our barn filled with pigeons, and I had them of every description, size, and color.

I was generally leading our "gang" into some new enterprise. Once it was a two-ringed circus, with a parade, clowns, the necessary monkey, and red lemonade. Another incident that I remember, and one that brought down the ire of my mother, was a game that I invented in the backyard. I never had much luck shooting marbles, so I worked out a scheme to get my share. I cut out the tops of several tomato cans, obtained some red paint and painted some round spots of the same size all over a board which had sides and a back; this board I placed against the barn about two feet higher than the ground. The game was three of the tomato can tops for a "crockey" or seven for a "flint"— that is, anyone who could stand back at the required distance and cover up one of the spots by pitching his tins would receive so many marbles reward. The news soon spread over the neighborhood, and within a few hours there were half a hundred boys of every size and color on hand. I was just in the midst of my triumph and had accumulated three or four boxes of marbles when my mother, seeing the swarming crowd, appeared, and in less time than it takes to tell it, there was not a boy in sight, my board was reduced to kindling wood, and the marbles were flying after the scurrying boys.

Some of my most interesting experiences in these early years happened in the days when I was a " newsie "—the first and only colored boy at the time on a route. This I had been able to purchase with money I had saved from the sale of rabbits and pigeons. It did not cost much, this route, but the experience it brought me—surpassing the lure and benefit of gold, shriving and fitting me for the arena of human action and struggle where no quarter is asked or given—can not be measured in dollars or cents. The paper was *The Press*, and the various boys handling the route had one by one got out of it all they could and then dropped it. The circulation manager, put to it, had picked up boys here and there as he could get them and thus the paper would often fail of delivery for days at a time. Sometimes, too, the boys would carry but a portion of the route, hiding the remainder of their papers under a bridge or even throwing them away. I made it a point to be on time each evening to obtain my papers, for it was fall and darkness came early. My father had taught me always to " be at the right place at the right time," and I realized that because of my race, to succeed I should be compelled to exhibit greater industry, efficiency, and intelligence than the white boys who had worked before me. I knew a boy who had a whistle made out of a piece of wood and I traded him a pigeon for it, and each evening when I threw the paper on a porch I would blow the whistle. Never an evening did I miss, regardless of cold or rain or snow, and never an evening did I fail to go to the end of my route, although the last mile had but two subscribers. Within a month I had sixty-four customers, and in the second month one hundred and twenty-eight, so that I was compelled to secure help to carry the papers part of the way.

It was about the time my route had grown to its greatest extent that one of the most pointed lessons of my life came to me. The paper, delivered, cost ten cents a week, and my customers were all of the working class; they largely did their business in units of nickels and dimes, and all planned to have their dimes ready on Saturday night. One bitterly cold Saturday night I had started unusually early to cover my route as there was to be an entertainment and festival at our church, and I was to meet my parents and sisters there. At the house next to the last the lady handed me a quarter. I reached in my pocket for the change, but to my great chagrin I could not find a cent. For a moment I was dumb. I searched again and in one of my pockets found a hole almost large enough for a quarter to go through, and I realized that I had left a trail of nickels and dimes behind me. I handed the quarter back to the lady saying I would collect for two weeks the coming Saturday night, and on my way to the last house a conflict raged in my mind as to what I should do. Against the lure of a trail of shiny nickels and dimes lost somewhere was that of the church gathering with the concert, the merry crowd, and the good things to eat. By the time I reached the house, however, my mind was made up: I must find that money, only a part of which belonged to me. I told the man in the house of my trouble and obtained from him the loan of a lantern, telling him to keep his dime in payment for his kindness. He said that were he I he would let the search go until morning; but he spoke to no avail. I knew the alleys, crosscuts, and yards through which I always went; I could trace them in the dark. After reaching the spot where the money had started filtering through my

LEARNING TO BE USEFUL

pocket I had found every nickel and dime less fifty-five cents, which I was sure people passing had picked up, the gaps in the silver trail being under the arc-lights. I had lost something—much to a struggling Negro boy pursued by suspicion; but I had also gained something—something far more valuable than gold and silver, and that has sustained my faith and strengthened my will through many dark days in life's problems.

It was shortly after this that I applied to Mr. Luther Perry, a colored man who ran a mattress factory a short distance from our home, for a job shaking out bales of excelsior. Mr. Perry was a good, clean man, a Sunday School superintendent, and he did not allow any swearing, smoking, or roughness of any kind about the place. I called for a bale and one was assigned to me. The bales weighed about five hundred pounds and were made of long strands of shavings tightly pressed together. The job was to pull the flakes apart and shake them out until no lumps remained. I worked faithfully that first evening, yet succeeded in getting only about one-third done. And what a pile it made, with two-thirds of the bale still before me! Worst of all, when I went back it looked as if someone had added about two-thirds more. Of course I was the laughing-stock of the place until my unenviable prominence was taken by another newcomer; but I soon became accustomed to the work and never again did I have to work a whole week for thirty cents.

I rejoice when I think of the fact that in old Missouri, a former slave state, the public library was open to all who had a mind to read; and there I spent many an hour that filled me with inspiration. I had also heard my mother speak of Boston and its wonderful schools and colleges. I felt that it must be the greatest place in the world—that all one had to do was to get there and all good and desirable things would be as free as the water of the rivers. The people there, it seemed, were standing ready and waiting to provide an education for all who knocked at their doors; there also all troubles would be over. One day I talked the matter over with myself and secretly decided to go there. I had eighteen dollars saved from shoe-shining and selling papers. I put this amount in my pocket, hid my books under the railroad bridge, and set out. My fare was paid to Rock Island; there I planned to stop and tell my Aunt Sally and Uncle Charley good-bye. When I got there, however, I found that my father and mother, suspecting my destination, had wired them to look out for me. I did not get to Boston at this time, and in general my visits in these years were divided between this home and that of my Aunt Dot and Uncle Bill, who lived not far away at Cedar Rapids. Aunt Dot was prone to make a real pet out of any child about her, and it is likely that I should have grown lazy enough had it not been for one thing. Uncle Bill was an engineer and worked in all sorts of fascinating places; he was engineer and foreman at the electric light plant and fireman at Averill's Wagon Plant, the son and the daughter of the owner of which place are now very loyal supporters of the Piney Woods School. Uncle Bill was a jovial man and liked to talk; he permitted me to go with him to his work, and the way he always explained the machinery to me made me love it and also taught me to realize how wonderful a thing a machine can be. After a while he went to Marshalltown, Iowa, and that is how it happened that I entered the high school in this place. I was encouraged to go also by the fact that I learned that there was a restaurant there kept by a colored man with whom I might find work. I found " Bob's Place," as I had expected, and there I worked for a couple of years; but the red demon whiskey got the better of Bob, his place became a little rowdy and business declined, and so I sought and found work at the Pilgrim Hotel.

It was during my high-school days in Marshall-town that my first realization of the work young white men were doing came to me. One young man who was a bell-boy in the hotel where I worked for my room and board, was promoted to the position of night clerk. No one knew whence he had come and he had not even finished the grammar school. At that time the position of night clerk in the Pilgrim Hotel looked pretty big to me, and I wondered if I could hope for such a promotion after I finished my course. My own regular work was to help the girls in the dining-room. I assisted at breakfast until 8.50, then hastened to school; came back at noon and worked until 1.10, and then helped with supper in the evening. At night I was on the lookout for an opportunity to make a little extra money for my expenses, and because of this I worked at nearly everything about the hotel. When a bell-boy, porter, fireman, dish-washer, or bootblack wanted an evening off or was ill, I usually worked in his place. Quite often I was called out to serve parties in the town, and I also had the job of swinging the front door for the members of the Twentieth Century Club at their monthly meetings, for which I received a dollar an evening, and, best of all, a chance to hear the programs.

The coming of two young men, Ellis U. Graff, as principal of the high school, and William I. Crane, as superintendent of schools, gave me a new knowledge of what young white men were doing. We had heard a great deal of how Mr. Crane had built up the schools in another place; he gave a series of lectures at the court house which, altogether, made us look upon him very much as the people did the schoolmaster in " The Deserted Village," and wonder how " one small head could carry all he knew." Mr. Graff brought youth, enthusiasm, and an unusual sympathy. I remember once carrying to him a clipping of the Socialist platform and asking him to explain it to me. He took it and told me to come in after school was over; when I did he had carefully written out an explanation of each article. I marveled that he should give so much time and attention to me, for previous principals that I had known were rather rough and unsympathetic. Later, having heard that Dr. Crossland, of St. Joseph, had been appointed Minister to Liberia, I wondered, not being acquainted with the game of politics, whether I could become his secretary, as I had once been a collector for him. I told Mr. Graff of my aspiration; he encouraged me and said that my application could not do any harm, and that at least I should gain by writing it.   Of course I received an answer that the appointment had been made.

On Mr. Graff's recommendation I was asked to be grammar grade editor of the *Quill*, our little high-school paper. This necessitated my visiting the grade schools and explaining that we wanted to have them represented with monthly notes. At one school the principal asked me to explain the matter to three or four of the higher classes. Thus I made my first speeches.

For my share of the Commencement program at the end of the course I was assigned the pleasant task of writing the class song. While I was waiting for the Muse to inspire me the others of the class began to get nervous, and some even went to the principal to lay the matter before him. The next day one of the boys asked me about the song and told me that they were a little worried and had consulted Mr. Graff about what to do. I asked what he had said, and was informed that he had laughed and remarked, "Oh! Jones will come up with it all right." This was a revelation to me. For the first time I realized that someone had confidence in me. I can not explain the new lease of life I took. I should have written that song or died in the attempt, and the next morning I had it ready. When the diplomas were being given out at Commencement and it came my turn to walk across the stage and receive mine, the opera house burst into applause and I nearly fainted with fright. That night in my little room in the basement of the hotel it dawned upon me that as I was the first colored graduate of the Marshalltown High School the people had their eyes upon me, and I felt that I must now make good in one way or another. That was in 1903.

While in Marshalltown I always looked forward to Sunday with a special degree of pleasure; first, because the day meant the coming of several of the townspeople to dinner and that meant extra tips, and, second, because there were the afternoon meetings at the Y. M. C. A. In St. Joseph the color of my skin had been a bar against joining or visiting the Young Men's Christian Association. Aside from the churches there was no place to which to go on Sunday afternoons except the ball games, amusement parks, or on railway excursions. In Iowa everything was different. The doors of the Y. M. C. A. swung wide open for any young man who would live in a clean, wholesome atmosphere. I soon became a member, and the swimming pool, the reading-room, and the gymnasium allured me at all idle times. Here for the first time on Sunday afternoons I heard big, strong young men under the leadership of our boyish hero, S. W. Fellingham, stand up and in no uncertain terms acknowledge the fatherhood of God and the leadership of Jesus Christ. How I enjoyed and received strength from those Sunday afternoon meetings!

I had graduated from the high school, but I realized that I knew but little, so I determined to enter a business college while deciding how I should continue my regular school work. Accordingly, at the Central Iowa Business College I secured a job as janitor which would pay for my tuition while I could still work for my room and board at the hotel. Here I met the principal, Mr. W. H. Gilbert, a young man who was running a large business college in a businesslike way, but who was never too busy to explain any difficulty. During the summer, while I was waiting at table one noon, Mr. Graff and a number of men were seated at my table. As they were getting up Mr. Graff introduced me to a Mr. Chesney from the State University. Mr. Chesney smiled, acknowledged the introduction, and told me that the University was just the place at which I should finish my education, and said that he had no doubt that as I worked my way tuition would be remitted. Later I had a conference with Mr. Graff and came

Winter and the Woodpile
First Corn of the Season

to the decision to enter the institution in the fall. I was further encouraged in this decision by Mrs. Richard Lane, now of Davenport, who gave me a letter to a member of the Beta Theta Pi Fraternity which secured for me there a place where I could work for my room and board. Accordingly, after the county superintendent, Miss Hostettler, had signed certain papers necessary for having my tuition remitted, I set out for Iowa City. I soon became a real freshman; and my desire for elevation in the mental world was reinforced from a physical standpoint, for my room at the club house was in one corner of the attic, and I was now higher above the ground than I had been below the ground at Marshalltown, and could but smile at my good fortune. During my sophomore year I met in class a young man, Mr. Frederick R. Cooper, whom I soon grew to like because of his friendliness and our interest in the same things, and for my last two years in Iowa City I worked at his fraternity, the Delta Tau Delta. My university day usually started at 4.30 in the morning, when I would build a fire in the furnace, and I could hardly reach my room at night before nine o'clock; then I would be busy with the preparation of my work for the next day until eleven or twelve o'clock.

During my sophomore year I heard our President, Dr. George E. MacLean, use the phrase, "Noblesse Oblige," and one day in the botany class Professor Thomas H. MacBride explained to me its meaning. More than ever I realized that because of the superior advantages for schooling that had been mine, I was morally obligated to pass the opportunity on to those less fortunate than myself. I believe I had always had a subconscious desire to be a school teacher, but I had also cherished a desire to engage in the poultry business. One of my fondest dreams was to realize money enough from this business some day to cross the ocean and see the countries of the Old World. "Noblesse Oblige," however, taught me that my duty was down in the black belt among the less fortunate of my people.

This conviction came to me strongly in my junior year through the "Industrial Art" class work of Professor Clark Fisher Ansley. It was seminar work, and during the latter half of the year I was assigned the task of developing a theme on the work of Dr. Booker T. Washington. I proceeded to read and re-read this leader's books and to look up every magazine article listed in the various indexes. The result was that I got together an interesting amount of material and for the first time realized the meaning of the poet's phrase, "Our echoes roll from soul to soul," when I learned that Mark Hopkins taught General S. C. Armstrong, and that General Armstrong taught and inspired Booker T. Washington. Most of the class members had been given an hour each to the topics assigned, but I was so full of my subject that I was given six hours. A member of the class who was on the staff of the city papers gave a review of each lecture to the various papers. I called the attention of the class to the fact that the Negro race had many other great men, distinguished in various lines, who simply happened not to be so well known as Dr. Washington. One of the highest expressions of Negro life and achievement, I said, was to be found in the life, personality, and writings of Dr. W. E. B. DuBois. From industrial training to the scholarship of Dr. DuBois seemed a long step, but it showed the possibilities of the Negro. I further said that Dr. DuBois was not opposing industrial education but that his great contention was that there was not so much a "Negro Problem" as a "Human Problem," as Frederick Douglass once said, and that industrial education was no more a means for the complete development of the Negro than any other kind of education. I also read some passages from the beautiful and fascinating "Souls of Black Folk," which book so impressed me that I decided to purchase a copy and present it to my English teacher, Miss Mary G. Chawner, in appreciation of the interest and help she had given me in my courses.

A short while after this another of my teachers, Miss Leona Call, who was president of the First Baptist Church Missionary Society, asked me to talk on the condition of my people in the South. The day of the meeting I met a young colored woman, Miss Grace M. Allen, who was in town in the interest of an industrial school in the South. I asked her to attend the meeting and contribute something from her experience. So she did, and I thought her the brightest and most enthusiastic little woman of my race that I had ever met. I saw in her my ideal and felt sure that we should meet again some day—and we did.

During my last two summers in Iowa City I realized my Pilgrim Hotel ambition by becoming a night clerk at one of the local hotels. Several of the guests registered their prejudice by going to the landlord, but he told them that he was running the hotel, and I went on with my work. One evening at the close of my senior year—commencement week, 1907—while I was waiting at table, a gold watch was presented to me by the members of the Delta Tau Delta Fraternity; and next to the ovation given me in Marshalltown this was the greatest surprise of my life. Then came commencement day and with it the Secretary of War, William Howard Taft, who delivered the graduation address. Once more I had completed a prescribed course of study. Once more I looked out upon the world and realized how little I really knew.

III

PINE-KNOTS AND THE BLUE SKY

WHY in the world did you ever go South?" is the common query when I journey North. To most of my friends the North is still the land of opportunity as well as freedom, and they hardly see how one can exist elsewhere. Almost unconsciously, however, I had decided to go South. Perhaps this was my modernized version of "Go West, young man," yet as the years have passed I have come to see in it more clearly the hand of God who had heard the cries of my people in the woods for the opportunities of education which were being denied them. At any rate I packed my trunk, and without notifying relatives or friends, I set out. I first went to Arkansas to become used to the Southern climate. Here I found a job looking after a horse and carriage and milking a cow. Meanwhile I was in correspondence with Dr. Booker T. Washington's great Tuskegee Institute and was in line for a place there, but decided to go to a little school in

Hinds county, Mississippi, an outgrowth of Tuskegee. The salary was smaller, but somehow it seemed that greater good could be done there.

Christmas of the second year I spent at the plantation home of one of my students, who was from the Piney Woods of Mississippi near Braxton, which is in that part of the state between Jackson and Gulfport, on the Gulf and Ship Island Railway.

And what a holiday season it was! As elsewhere in the South, " taking Christmas " was one continuous round of fireworks, frolicking, feasting, and preaching services that sometimes lasted throughout the day and that were interrupted only by the calls to the well-laden tables just outside the church. At the time of my visit a district Sunday School convention was in session, and I was asked to speak each day. I learned that the convention had been organized twenty-five years before and that its aim was to build a high school. By this was meant a school that would carry the boys and girls to what in the North are termed the seventh and eighth grades. The little rural schools were many miles apart, and the teachers were not paid over an average of $18.00 a month, and hardly measured up to Northern boys and girls in the fifth and sixth grades. One teacher often had as many as sixty or seventy pupils. The school-houses were unceiled, black with soot, without glass windows, and with no blackboards. A high school had been a forlorn hope; no one seemed to know just what to do, and the mites brought together from time to time rarely amounted to more than twelve dollars. The sincerity of the people, however, and their regular meetings from year to year, with the steady gaze upon the star of hope, impressed me greatly.

The evening of the first Christmas that I spent in the Piney Woods strengthened my desire to cast my lot there. Through the great dark woods by the light of a pine torch we were taken to a frolic. In a close room, filled with tobacco smoke and reeking with the odor of whiskey, a crowd of men, women, and children, laughing and joking, jostled and danced to the music of an old guitar until early morning. Occasionally someone would step outside and with a succession of shots satisfy himself as to how quickly he could pull the trigger. This program continued for a week at one place and then the crowd moved on to the next cabin.

I cornered the men in one room when they came out for a rest and talked " school," but was answered by the remark that their convention had been trying to build a school for twenty years, but

COMING TO ENTER PINEY WOODS

Bringing Her Grandson.

Mother Brings Fruit and Geese to Pay Her Daughter's Entrance Fee.

Mother and Daughter, with all Her Earthly Possessions under Her Arm.

Father Bringing Son and Mattress and a Load of Corn to Pay for His Schooling.

that the boll-weevil was on hand, so " it wouldn't be much use trying." The children seemed to enjoy the frolic quite as much as the older people. They swore just as wickedly, and even the boys and girls nine years of age used quantities of snuff and tobacco. Their parents thought that anything, even liquor, if used by themselves, was all right for the children; so it was only necessary to ask " Pa " for what was wanted. In general, however, I found the moral condition of the people much higher than I had expected to find it. Those who respected the bonds of matrimony were greatly in the majority and looked with disfavor upon improper conduct of any kind. On my last night I sat among a group of these people and in the soft glow of a great pine-knot fire I told them of how the people farmed and lived in Iowa, of how the boys and girls were educated, how they celebrated Christmas; and I promised that later I would come back and see if in any way I could help them.

In May, after the closing of school in Hinds county, I set out again for the Piney Woods. My two years in the South had earned $490 and my living. I had been able to make the $90 do for expenses and had invested the $400 in land, almost the last money I had being paid on this. I had enough left to pay my way to Jackson, and there

I pawned my watch for $2.50. My fare to Brax-
ton was 85 cents; so when I arrived I had only
$1.65 in cash with which to begin work. The hos-
pitable people were glad to see me, however, and
made me welcome.

I went to work immediately, visiting in the
homes, in the churches, in neighborhood meetings,
and under the trees at noontime—anywhere I could
get a few together. I saw that the future of the
majority of the people must be as country-folk,
and that to make them a better country-folk was
the task of their helper. It was clear that the base
of operation must be in the kitchen, the household,
the garden, and the farm. So I talked diversified
farming and around the firesides at night we fig-
ured out the cost of raising ten-cent cotton and
buying fifteen-cent bacon and ninety-cent corn
from the meat-houses and corncribs of the North
I showed the folly of saving the worst land for
the corn crop, from which they must derive their
living, and of going to the crib in the spring and
picking up anything left for seed corn, instead of
selecting their seed in the field. Better stock and
poultry, and everything pertaining to better farming, was talked of and illustrated with a *Wallace's
Farmer, Successful Farming,* and such Southern
farm papers as I could get hold of. Meanwhile in

the homes I told the women about sanitary cooking and whitewash, and sometimes I applied the whitewash myself.

In this way I traveled all over Rankin county and a part of Simpson, sometimes astride a mule, sometimes in an ox-wagon, but more often afoot, sometimes walking eighteen or twenty miles a day. I had been in one place, Taylor Hill community, only a few days when I found it necessary late one afternoon to see a man who lived in another settlement. The pleased-looking old man of whom I asked the way told me that it was out Big Woods way "a li'l' piece yon side de creek." I could not miss it, he said. "Go dis way, turn on dis han' side," indicating which hand; "keep on like dat twell you come to de forks o' de road, take de dis han' form," again indicating which hand he meant, "an' follow on twell you come to de creek. Dar you'll fin' a foot bridge. Cross over. Take out thoo de woods an' keep de path twell you come to anothern on dis han' side; turn off an' follow on twell fus thing you knows you's dar."

Trying to remember his instructions I managed to reach the creek. Night had already come among the deep woods all around, but against the dim gleam of the water I made out the darker silhouette of the " bridge," once a conveniently situated tree which had fallen so as to reach from bank to bank. The bridge looked long, and oh! how narrow; and the water beneath it looked as though it might be mysteriously and dangerously deep, full of hidden depths and holes and quick-sands. Gladly would I have turned back, but I did not dare, for while my directions had brought me thus far forward I could not think of where they might lead me should I reverse and try to work them backwards; and it was certain that I could not stay where I was all night. So I started across, and the farther I went the narrower seemed the bridge, until when I was about halfway the only way I could find room for my feet was by keeping them close one behind the other. Once my hand touched something cold and clammy, but whatever it was—frog or lizard or something else —so rapidly was I advancing that it is likely the force of our collision stunned it for life. " Take out thoo de woods an' keep de path twell you come to anothern on dis han' side. Take dat an' follow on twell all at once you's dar." After crossing the bridge I followed or thought I followed the direc-tions, but after quite a tramp I found myself at another creek. I turned back, tramped further and came to another. This happened again and again until it was borne upon my excited mind that all these were not different creeks but just one creek, a mysterious one indeed, running in the shape of a perfect letter O, and I by a terrible mistake had got on the island in its center; and there was no way out. Panic seized me. I tore through brush and tangle, stumbling and panting, not knowing whither I fled. Heavy darkness enfolded me and all the terrors of the woods surrounded me. The place seemed fairly to breathe with horrors, and then the low weird sighing night wind that sprung up and the chill that came with it took from me the last vestige of reason and strength. I realized that I was doomed and dropped down from sheer exhaustion. But I would not give up. I started out again; for hours I hunted a way out, and then I dropped down exhausted again, for how long a time I do not know. And then I heard a bird singing, not screeching or groaning, but singing. A grayness stole through the woods; almost before I knew it all the glory of dawn was in the sky. Vanishing with the darkness went all my fears and confusion. I realized that the creek was not shaped like an O, but that I had been traveling in a circle myself and had been coming back to the same spot all the time.

At that period of my existence, when I was still not long out of college, I was great on musing and moralizing, and just a few days later I used this incident in a speech to illustrate how my people were in the darkness of ignorance with all its superstition and fears, and how they needed light, and how the light was sure to come. Another time I lost my way and wandered into a part of Smith county where there were no colored people. I walked all day hoping that I should come to a settlement. I had nothing to eat with me, and not knowing what fate might overtake a strange Negro if he stopped to ask questions I journeyed on drinking from the brooks and eating such berries as I could find in the woods. It was long after dark before I saw the first cabin in a colored settlement, the firelight shining between the cracks in the logs. To my "Hello" the familiar "Who dat?" told me that I had reached a haven of rest, and that the next night I should have those about me to tell about the high school that they were to help build.

Thus I studied the people and the country, and the entire summer was spent in this way. In the fall I found that I was no better off financially than when I first entered the Piney Woods. On Sundays at their meetings the people would take up an after collection for the "Fesser"—generally eighty or ninety cents, but often only fifteen or twenty cents, and with this I met the few current expenses I had.

About the first of October, having covered considerable territory and worn out the only shoes and clothing I had, I found myself back at Braxton, determined to begin the operation of a school. Although I was full of enthusiasm and had stirred up some degree of interest among both the white and the colored people, I realized the difficulty of making a start; but I had burned my bridges behind me and was determined to do or be found trying.

It had been the poorest crop season in the history of the country, with rain, rain, rain. The merchants had put out money for provisions and clothing for the colored people, as is the custom in the South, and it looked as if there would be no cotton with which to pay because of the continuous rains. I talked the matter over with Mr. Mangum, the cashier of the Braxton Bank, who is now our treasurer, and in his kindly, sympathetic way he said, " Well, Jones, the outlook is rather gloomy; it looks like the rain has the best of us; my money's out, the darkies are all blue, and I'm blue, so that we're about one color; but go ahead and do what you can and I'll help you a little later." Another local white man, Mr. J. R.

Webster, I found at his mill checking up lumber. He said that an industrial school for the colored people was a fine thing and that he would give some lumber when it got started. He also allowed me the use of his typewriter.

I had some interesting experiences with the local Church Association, Sunday School Convention, and such organizations. For the meetings of these bodies the people sometimes drive forty or fifty miles, coming in wagons or buggies or on mules to the great event of the year. Those who can not find places to stay near the church camp out in the open. There are tables and counters and vendors out under the trees, where are sold hot fish, oranges, apples, soda water, crackers, and anything else the appetite might call for. In the church and around the doors and windows are the older people. Next is a circle of young people walking to and fro. It is their great social time of the year; every girl must have a new calico dress for the occasion and every boy a new suit, and many a court-ship that ends in marriage begins at the " Associa-tion." On the edge of the crowd are the tables and stands, while surrounding all is the circle of wagons and buggies and mules. The buggies fur-nish convenient places for the young people to sit and court. Beyond all else are the camp followers,

First Graduating Class

Early Faculty

horse traders and the fellows with a little "blind tiger" whiskey. It seems impossible to keep them away, and often there are as many white men as colored in this gang.

During the month of August the Spring Hill Association was to have its annual meeting, each church being represented by two delegates and four dollars in money, with instructions as to the division of this money between the funds for Education, Home Missions, Foreign Missions, and Superannuated Ministers. My friends were all in a great state of preparation for the gathering, and several advised that I should go by all means. It was a hot, dusty August day when we started upon our twenty-mile journey over a narrow, rugged road, with roots and stumps and gullies and washed-out places at frequent intervals. I did not know that the young man with me had taken the old plug we were driving right off the pasture, that he had hitched him up without sufficient feed or water, or that he was old. At any rate his debilitated condition brought on colic and he died the day after we arrived at the Association. This was only the beginning of trouble. The members of the Association could not exactly understand my mission among them, and those who were at the head of affairs were as jealous of their positions as if they had been rulers of principalities. They did not know but that I was a preacher in disguise, they did not permit me to come before the body or take any part in the proceedings, and I found myself completely "frozen out" on a sizzling August day. When the meeting was over and the tents were being taken down and the stands knocked to pieces, everybody seemed in a hurry to leave. Buggies and wagons were soon hitched up and the people climbed in and rumbled off down the roads in clouds of dust but not one seemed going in my direction. Wearily I turned back toward my settlement with a twenty-mile walk before me. When I arrived I found that the news of the death of the old horse was already there. The young man had not returned with me. Not relishing the idea of facing his people without the horse, he had decided to visit a few days before returning, so that the death of old Doc was entirely upon my own shoulders although I was only a guest and had not in any way assumed the responsibility of driving the horse. My stock dropped to zero, things were dark and ominious, and failure stared me in the face. Then I remembered hearing some of my University teachers tell about Mark Twain and Walter Scott, who had been connected with companies that failed and who while they were not under any responsibility from a purely business standpoint to stand for the losses of the others in the company, nevertheless because of the moral consideration paid back every dollar their defunct companies owed. I felt I should do the same, for I did not want to fail in my object of educating these people. I did not want to leave with this odium upon me and I certainly would not climb to success over the misfortune of the lowliest in the Black Belt. As the owner and I could not agree on the value of the plug, we each selected a man, and the two selected a third who would act with them as a committee to fix the value of the animal. The verdict was for $125, which amount was really $75 more than the horse was worth. I said I would pay the sum with the first money I could earn. My good friend, Mr. Taylor, however, who had been my nominee, came to the rescue and loaned the money upon my word, without security of any kind. My stock again rose rapidly, and I have never regretted the decision to do more than I was morally responsible for. I had helped to build up my credit not only in Braxton, but in Jackson as well; and some of the very people who looked askance now came around and said that I had been overcharged. Since then the owner of the horse has moved to Louisiana, and for two years he sent his youngest son back to the Piney Woods School. In 1919 the young man was graduated as the valedictorian of his class, and he married one of the graduates of 1918.

Another organization in the county known as the St. John's Semi-Annual Convention, the president of which had first invited me down, was my next hope of getting a start. This would not budge. The president was accused of bringing down a " furiner " to take away their convention from them, and a new president was elected. The treasurer was opposed to any forward movement because he had used up the $75 or $80 in the treasury and was not in a position to replace this. Still another of the leaders had some boys who had been sent away to school and who were now rural teachers, and he was not willing to boost anything of which they could not be the head. In general the opinion was, " We have been laboring for twenty years to build a high school, and if we go ahead and let Fesser Jones build one under our authority he'll get the praise." A little later I attended a smaller convention. Here one of the leading lights remarked, " I wish that feller 'ud go on away from here; he's got too much sense. I know he'd never come away down here with his sense fer any good to us." It must be remembered that I had friends in all of these meetings who were willing to do for me anything they could, but the moderators and other officers had a sort of interlocking directorate and they did not want it disturbed, school or no school. The more I thought of the matter the more certain was I that I ought to be able to do something for these people out in the great Piney Woods, and I finally came to the conclusion that the start must be made in some other way. I had been accustomed to go to a spring on an old farm about two miles from where I was staying to read and write under a large cedar tree. One afternoon while I was at this place day-dreaming there came to my mind the saying that Mark Hopkins on one end of a log and a student on the other would constitute a university, and I thought that surely I ought to be able to teach these illiterate boys and girls without the formality of buildings and desks and blackboards. So the inspiration came to me to open school under the old cedar tree, in God's out-of-doors, with His vast blue dome for our schoolhouse, and I set out to notify the farmers around that school would open on the next Monday morning at the cedar tree on the old Mordecai Harris place.

Many of them had already laughed at me for

sitting around the old place and now they laughed anew. The very idea of starting a high school under a tree—impossible! This only strengthened my determination, however. On Monday morning three boys met me, and a few of the old brethren. We assembled under the tree on some pine logs, and after singing " Praise God from whom all blessings flow," reading lessons from the Bible, and offering prayer, declared school open.

The next day I had a few more students, and the number grew until there were some twenty-nine. Each new addition meant more pine logs for seats. After a few weeks two of the students, a young man and a young woman whom I had taught before coming to the Piney Woods, joined me, and several more insisted upon coming though I had no place for them to stay. The young man was a very good carpenter and the young woman fairly well advanced in her studies. They became my efficient assistants. It was now November and the days were a little chilly. We would each build a bonfire and roll our logs around and thus hear the classes. In the meantime the recess period was spent in hewing out benches. Near by our open-air school was an old tumble-down cabin in which a drove of sheep took shelter. It was also inhabited by lizards, snakes, and owls, and was almost hid-

(Above) *"Farmers' Conference."* E. R. Harlan, Curator of Iowa Historical Society, Speaker of the Day, in Front Line.

(Below) *"Bringing the North and South Together."* Domestic Science Department serves a dinner at a Farmers' Conference for northern and southern white friends and Trustees. At head of table on left: Major R. W. Millsaps, Miss.; on right: Professor P. G. Holden of Iowa. To right of Professor Holden: Captain Asa Turner and Hon. W. P. Mangum of Miss. on left front end.

den by the weeds that had grown up around it. I made some inquiries and found that it, as well as the land we were on, belonged to an aged colored man by the name of Taylor, who the people said was the only one among them who could do anything, but who was mean and stingy so that it would be useless to see him. I asked where he lived and started out to find him, and I met him out in a field plowing with an old mule. I hailed him and introduced myself. He said that he had heard of me, that it looked as though I meant business, and that if I would wait a few minutes he would " take out " and talk. This I did, and then we went to his cabin. He explained that he had let everything run down as he was planning to leave the country and go West, and did not want to leave anything behind. He had had interesting experiences. He had gone with Major Palmer after the war to Rockford, Ill., and had obtained three terms of schooling at the little red schoolhouse near Cherry Valley, and later had lived in Keokuk, Iowa, where he worked as a barber. Then he had returned to his old state of Mississippi and by virtue of the education he had received had been able to buy several hundred acres of land and save a little money. We talked until three o'clock in the morning, and he decided to give forty acres of land and fifty dollars in money toward the substantial beginning of the school. The next day we went down and looked over the forty acres, and the following Saturday he went to town and deeded the property to the trustees of the Piney Woods Industrial School and gave a check for fifty dollars.

Here was a man different from any colored man I had yet met in the Piney Woods. The following Sunday he and I visited the local church to announce the gift and to see what we could do to stir up some enthusiasm. After the meeting, being given an opportunity to speak, I announced the great gift of Mr. Taylor, whereupon one of the deacons jumped up and said, " I ain't goin' to have nothin' to do with it. There's some trick about it; Taylor never would have done that if it wasn't a trick." This outburst considerably dampened the feeling. Mr. Taylor had been so good and kind to me, however, that my fighting blood had been aroused, and I declared that he and I were more determined than ever to build a school and that we intended to proceed with the work even if we had to go forward alone. Mr. Taylor then stood up and emphasized what I had said, and the meeting closed in a blaze of enthusiasm.

Next day I rode around through the settlement

to find out what each would do. Some pledged a
little money, the highest amount being the $15 of
Hector McClaurin, one of the most substantial
farmers. Others said they would help haul the
lumber, some said they would help in the building,
while still others said they would help " rive out
de bods." I did not know just what that had to
do with building a school but thought if it would
help any I should be glad to see it done.

I was now happier than I had ever been before
in my life. We set to work, floored the old cabin,
put a dirt and stick chimney at each end, and
whitewashed it inside and outside. The result was
that the people said it looked better than it had
ever looked before in the half-century of its existence. In one side the young man, Yancy, and
myself fixed our living quarters, and the other side
became the schoolhouse. It was seven rooms in
one, serving as chapel, study hall, recitation room,
office, sewing room, carpenter shop and basket-
making shop as occasion required.

One day a friend, Tom Dixon, came to me and
said, " Mr. Jones, we are due a little schooling
from the county, and if you could get that you
would have a little something to help you." I
made inquiry and found that the county had been
accustomed to granting a three or four months

school, the length of the term and the salary (generally $15 or $18 a month) being dependent upon the pleasure of the superintendent. To get charge of the school would require two things, permission from the local trustees and then from the super-intendent. For several days I wrestled with the three trustees; one evening one would assent and as soon as I left him he changed his mind. Said one: "Fesser, suppose de projuct youse gitting up busts; den we'll be widout our school case it'll be part of youall's projuct, an' I'll be ter blame by de peoples." The next morning I once more had this one in the mood to go, but I was careful not to leave him again. We hitched up a mule and started by the home of one of the other men. This man we had to "get fixed" again; then it took him another hour to hitch up his mule and tie the harness together. At last, however, we were off to Brandon, seventeen miles away. We arrived just as the board was about to convene, and we happily succeeded in our errand.

We next called a great meeting of the people. Some eleven hundred came afoot, on horseback, in ox-wagons and vehicles of every description. Among them were the best white people from Braxton, three miles away. I remember Hon. R. F. Everett, president of the Braxton Bank, and some twenty-five others. The result of the meeting was a subscription list headed by the $50 of the ex-slave, Taylor, liberal gifts from the white friends, and the mites of the farmer folk, some of whom were able to give only a few pennies. Altogether we had enough to start a building. Then followed gifts of all sorts. Mr. Webster gave the lumber promised and we set a day to begin work; one good old woman brought two geese across the country. Such was the spirit in which the little school in the Piney Woods was started.

On the appointed day, after Scripture reading and prayer, some started to haul lumber while others got the ground ready for the foundation. In my overalls I helped swing the axes and pull the crosscut saw that felled the first tree. From day to day the farmers' wives would come at noon and bring baskets of food, and we would all rest in the shade of the trees until time to go back to work. During the rest period I would conduct a farmers' experience meeting. At night, after the others had gone back to their homes, Yancy and I would continue to work until dark. Then we would go to our cabin and prepare supper.

We progressed rapidly with the building, and soon had the framing up and the weather-boarding on. Then one night a terrible gulf-storm blew across the state, uprooting trees, destroying houses and livestock, and leaving death and destruction in its wake. As we lay on our cots in the old cabin, praying that our lives might be saved, we could hear the snapping of the gigantic pines and the crashing of timber and buildings blown about the country. The flashes of lightning were dazzling and the thunder was deafening, and the cabin groaned and trembled beneath the shock of the trees and timber blown against it. When we saw the wreckage the next morning the fact that we were alive and the cabin still standing was to me a manifestation of the power of prayer. The top of our cedar tree had been blown off and everywhere the pines were in a broken tangle, and our building, while not blown down, was off its foundation and almost wrecked.

This misfortune nearly disheartened me. It was the most discouraging thing that had yet come into my life. I walked around the building several times trying to realize whether I was awake or dreaming. It all proved to be no dream; so we borrowed some jacks from the mills and railroad company and set to work to put the whole back in shape. After the farmers had straightened up their fences they flocked to help us; even the women came and helped to clear away the debris.

(Top)   Mother's Club, Organized by Mrs. Jones.
(Below)   "Clearing the Land" Principal Jones leading his school boys
ling trees for the first building.   All buildings even the late brick ones a
nstructed by students.

After days of toil and sleepless nights we finally succeeded in getting the building together and back on its original foundation, and everyone declared that it looked as well as before, if not better. We worked on and finally were able to move into our new building, which was dedicated and named "Taylor Hall," in honor of the man who had given the first money toward its erection. The old cabin now served only for sleeping quarters and the office.

We closed the year free from debt and had an average of eighty-five students. We had taught common English branches and sewing, basketry, broom-making and woodwork. There was also a beginning in flower gardening. Our closing exercises consisted of essays on housekeeping, cooking, sewing, gardening, and manual training.

There was no money for salaries and what donations we could get were used for the building up of the school. After school was out I succeeded in getting enough money together to send out a thousand circular letters. From all of them I received but one response. It was as follows: "Although I am helping all of the schools I can and do not want to take on any new obligations, your literature and story appeals to me in a special way. Enclosed, etc.—Emily Howland." This contribution

I felt was providential for it strengthened our faith that friends would come to our rescue and that we only needed to stay on the firing line. During the vacation we worked on, trying to make a little crop with our hands, for we had not a single animal to use for working the soil. Again we sent out a thousand circular letters, this time mostly to Iowa. Again among the thousand we found only one response. We opened a letter one morning and found in it a little pink check and these words: " I like what you are doing in your corner of the vineyard. May the Lord give you the desire of your heart. Enclosed, etc.—Asa Turner." Since then we have heard from this friend many times and have found him the kindest, most lovable man in all the world. Like the Master before him he goes about the world doing good. But who that knows anything about the history of Iowa does not know of Father Turner?

IV

LOG CABIN DAYS

I AM not sure just what we should call the first stage of the growth of the Piney Woods School, but I do know that the second stage might well be termed "Log Cabin Days."

When we had finished our first year of work it was more than ever necessary for us to try to place our effort before the public. I shall never forget my first days in Keokuk, where I was soliciting for the first time in my life. I arrived on Saturday afternoon, and on my way up from the depot I passed a broom factory. After I deposited my luggage at my rooming-place I returned to this factory to see what I could learn in the course of the afternoon about making brooms. I also learned that a set of broom machinery was not in use and would be sold reasonably. This I considered fortunate, for I wanted to install broom-making and I should now have something tangible to work for. On Sunday I visited several churches. At one I was allowed to tell my story before a large Bible

class though no collection was permitted. After
the class was dismissed, however, one man who was
interested came around and slipped a dollar into
my hand and gave me the names of some others
upon whom I might call the next day. The next
morning I went first to see Mr. Lee Hammill,
whom I was told that I must by all means visit
if I expected to have any luck in Keokuk. I
found him busy at his desk in the midst of a dozen
busy clerks. He gave me a sympathetic hearing,
remembered " Uncle Ed Taylor," who had bar-
bered there with an old Frenchman, and told me
that he had always felt compassion for the colored
people and was pleased to help, but that I must
first see a Mr. Huiskamp and whatever this man
did he would do also. I spent the rest of the day
trying to find Mr. Huiskamp and finally saw him
in his factory. He listened to me patiently and
then said that he had about " given out," and that
he now felt that for a while it was his first duty
to provide for his family. That evening I went
supperless to bed, but I could not rest. At last I
set my teeth and with a new determination got up
and dressed, and then I went out and looked up
the location of Mr. Huiskamp's residence. The
door was opened by the gentleman himself with a
paper in his hand. When he saw who I was and

I had begun talking about the school he said, "But I told you to-day that I could not do anything just now." I do not know what I said, or whether it was the haunting, determined look I had, but at last he told me to come back to his office the next day and he would do something. The next day I was up and at it again. I met another good friend in the person of Mr. G. Walter Barr, who encouraged me to go forward by declaring that I could not fail if I persisted. It took me nearly a week to raise the $35 to purchase the broom-making machinery which soon afterwards was on its way to the Piney Woods. The friendship thus formed for the school by Mr. Hammill and Mr. Barr has continued to grow and we have had the pleasure of thanking them many times for favors received.

From Keokuk I journeyed on to Des Moines, where my friend and fellow alumnus, Attorney S. Joe Brown, had arranged a meeting for me in the church of Dr. Howland Hanson, one of the largest in the city. Very few attended, but I raised a little money, secured some pledges, and, best of all, succeeded in getting my friend Brown to tell me of the mistakes I made. He emphasized the fact that the best part of my lecture was my own personal story of my work, and I have since found that he was entirely correct. While in Des Moines

I also met a young man, Louis Watson, who had attended the high school, but who had not been able to find anything other than the work of a porter to do. He was happy to cast his lot with us, and without a promise of salary began preparations to leave, despite the unfavorable comment of friends concerning the South.

We opened in the fall with five teachers. The young man who had been with us the first term had married during the summer and he brought his wife. She was to be a teacher for the extension work through the co-operation of the Anna T. Jeanes Fund. We enrolled over a hundred students and added a training kitchen for the girls. The money sent by Miss Howland we applied toward a little hand press and some type, and at the suggestion of this kind lady we began to print a little paper which we called *The Pine Torch*. Mr. Watson taught in the Academic Department and was also our official bookkeeper. He was one of the most faithful and conscientious young men it has ever been my good fortune to know. Often after teaching all day he would be bending over the books until after midnight. While we did not have a great deal of money to handle, we kept the work time of the students and also a careful record of their marks.

As Christmas time approached and the pitifully poor condition of the people began to impress itself upon Watson, he began to make plans for a real Christmas, such as he had been accustomed to see the children enjoy in the North. He sent to his mother for little candles and other decorations for a tree, and he set about making little Christmas boxes out of pasteboard and tissue paper, and painting motto cards for each of our students and for many of their parents. Time after time I remonstrated with him for working so steadily and keeping indoors so much, but he would only smile and answer that he wanted to let these poor boys and girls have a real Christmas for once in their lives, even if it was the last thing he ever did. So he worked on until late in the night, doing his regular work and painting the cards, and he was an excellent artist; and in the meantime the teachers prepared for a concert. The custom had been to have a great frolic to the accompaniment of an old guitar, with plenty to drink, fireworks and the shooting of pistols. This time we had a sermon in the afternoon, a sacred concert at night, and a Christmas tree gaily decorated and brilliant with dozens of candles. This was the first real Christmas the Piney Woods folk had ever witnessed, and how they enjoyed it, young and old! Not a gun was fired, not an unpleasant incident marred the blessed holiday; and how the eyes of the little boys and girls sparkled as they feasted upon the tree and as the names of the different ones were called for the boxes of nuts and candy! But alas for poor Watson! He had overworked himself, and the overwork, together with the poor food—for we subsisted mostly on cowpeas and cornbread—had taken all his strength. Within two weeks after Christmas, with a smile on his face, he went out, and the saddest thing I have ever had to do in life was to wire his mother about the return of her boy. His life was an inspiration for all of us, a benediction upon our work. We dedicated ourselves anew to the unfinished task that stretched before us and zealously turned again toward the sun.

Each day the students had worked half a day and gone to school half a day, and in this way we had cleared up a few acres of land, but we needed something to help with the plowing. A mule would cost $150, and the most we could raise was $20; so we bought a donkey that had been trained to plow, and though it was a rather slow proposition we set out to make a little crop. One day Mr. Taylor, returning from a trip to Jackson, told us about an old-style piano that he had seen for sale at $30. This was just $30 more than we had and the spring is a poor time for raising money in the South. But we needed music, and this piano was of just the kind and price for us. Finally one of our enthusiastic farmers, Amon Gipson, came to our rescue. He said he had been holding a bale of cotton and that he would sell it and go and get the piano for us, as he liked music and wanted to do something for the school each year. Accordingly we set out early one morning for Jackson, twenty-four miles away, with the bale of cotton, and returned with the piano, which has been of immeasurable help to us. Best of all, some eight months afterwards Mr. Gipson said to me: "Fesser Jones, I ain't never regretted I bought dat pianner fur de school. Od cose I only got fifty dollars fur my cotton, but I thought I'd manage to get along somehow, an' it seems dat since I done dat money has come to me an' I'se been able to get hold ob money dat I wouldn't have seen if I hadn't done dat. Yep, I'se powerful glad I done it."

The end of the school year came all too soon. Because the people are poor and do not use modern machinery everybody must work, and for this reason we set the closing date for the first week in May. Instead of a long series of essays and orations for our closing exercises, we attempted to show the people just what the students had been learning to try to make better their home-life. Mr. W. P. Mangum, the cashier of the Braxton Bank, had offered a gold medal to the girl who made the most progress in cooking, and as a part of the program the two girls who had made the highest marks in class cooked and served a meal before the audience. In judging the results the person of the girl, her care of the table, the floor, and the stove as well as the food were all taken into consideration. Another girl cut out and made a garment while the audience watched her. Another boy and girl set up in type some instructions to the farmers, and these another boy ran off on the little press. Still another boy had a pig that he exhibited to the audience, and he pointed out the difference between a good hog and the " razor-back, Piney Woods rooter." Both our white visitors and our own people were exceedingly happy and enthusiastic over this commencement program. We closed school again out of debt. Not any of us had drawn salaries, but we had received a living and had the satisfaction of knowing that we had tried to do a little good.

Our summer program was then made out. Two of the teachers were to stay, and with the help of a few students make a little farm and garden. Another I asked to spend the summer back in the forest among the people organizing rural school improvement associations, cooking classes, corn clubs, and poultry clubs. For each of these movements I made out the literature and we felt that if they were once established some good would come of them. This teacher spent the entire summer in the work; sometimes she was twenty or even thirty miles from a railroad.

I myself was to go North again and try to interest the people in Iowa in what we were trying to do. I had planned a little picture story of our work and had talked it over with the other teachers, but there was no extra money for having it done. I had asked the teachers especially to remember this need in their prayers for especially since the storm I had unbounded faith in the power of prayer. One morning the mail brought just one letter. It was from Mr. Arthur Cox, and contained a draft which enabled us to have the necessary cuts made and a little story of the work put into booklet form. Then I started upon my journey.

Two of the most important incidents of this summer occurred in Des Moines. Captain Asa Turner pledged a hundred dollars if the colored people in the city would subscribe the same amount.

This they readily did. The other helping hand was stretched out by the Des Moines *Register and Leader,* which made a feature story of the work. This was written by Mr. F. W. Beckman, now a teacher in the Iowa State College, and occupied the entire front page of the Sunday magazine section.

On the third Monday in October, 1911, we opened our third year with five teachers who were all young colored people under thirty years of age and who were determined to make their lives during the year count more than in any previous year of their history. On the opening day each boy and girl and each teacher stood up and told of the summer's work. One boy told of how with his knowledge of carpentry gained at the school he had built a little shed for his father. Another told of selecting seed corn and raising ten more bushels of corn on an acre than his father and neighbors had ever raised. A girl told of how she had gathered a neighbor's children together in a little school and taught them for nine weeks. Everybody, it seemed, had tried to do something for someone else during the summer and all pledged their faith anew to strive as never before to build up themselves and the little school in the Piney Woods. Miss Emily Howland, our good friend who had

Mrs. Laurence C. Jones

given us the money with which we had purchased our little press, sent for a report of the work, and being pleased with it, sent money with which to buy a larger press and more equipment so that we could publish *The Pine Torch* regularly each month and keep our friends informed of our progress. This was a great step forward.

About Christmas time I had another evidence of the power of prayer. We needed a typewriter and had not the means to get one. I had asked the Master to open the way and had thought it was to be by buying on the installment plan. On the morning on which I went to the post-office to buy a money order for the first payment I was handed a letter from the " Maple Leaf Farm." I eagerly tore it open to see what message of good cheer " Uncle Asa " was sending. To my surprise it contained an express bill for a modern typewriter that was on the road, a Christmas gift from himself, Hon. Henry Wallace, and others. Another desire had been fulfilled; another straw had demonstrated that the wind was blowing in our favor.

One other matter I must mention. It will be recalled that in my junior year in college I had been assisted at a meeting by a young woman who had had some experience in educational work. This was Miss Grace M. Allen, a graduate of the

Burlington High School, who, after conducting for three years a school of her own, traveled in the interest of the Eckstein-Norton School in Kentucky until this was merged with Berea, and who then studied for two years in the Department of Public Speaking at the Chicago Conservatory of Music. We were married soon after the close of my third year at Piney Woods, while I was on my trip North in interest of the school. "My little partner" has the faith that removes mountains, and it is largely by reason of her energy and skill, her devotion and enthusiasm, that we have been able to accomplish more within the last few years than in any previous years in the history of the school.

V

"MESSAGES OF HOPE"

FOR some time Taylor Hall and the log cabin had served for school building, chapel, dormitories, printing-office, and domestic science department. The good white people of Braxton, seeing our effort and desiring to show their appreciation, decided to build a girls' dormitory. Mr. J. R. Webster gave the framing and Messrs. W. P. Mangum, R. F. Everett and J. P. Cox furnished most of the means for finishing the structure, which we christened "Braxton Hall." This building is two stories high and accommodates about forty girls.

With the scraps that were left we were able to build a little one-room shop for manual training. The woods and a group of our farmer friends soon gave us another little log cabin shop for simple work in blacksmithing and broom-making. The two smaller buildings occupied the space to the right and left of the walk between Braxton Hall and Taylor Hall, while just to the southeast of

Taylor Hall stood the old cedar tree and the original log cabin. Across the road, on a slight elevation, we have erected a large barn with money sent us by our friend Mr. Arthur Cox, and here some of the boys stay when they can not find room elsewhere. These buildings are all neatly whitewashed and give the place the appearance of an institution.

I shall never forget the beginning of our fifth year. Mrs. Jones had told the people that I should be back for the opening day and there they were, hundreds of them, young and old, and some from far back in the woods, to greet me. In my talk I said to them, among other things: "To-day marks the beginning of the fifth year of this little school in the Piney Woods. In the glow of a bonfire five years ago, before we had adequate shelter, I saw many of your faces light up with a new understanding of the meaning of education as we studied our books and practised our manual training. * * * A song you have just finished typifies the spirit of this institution more than anything else I know of. Well may you sing 'Keep Inchin' Along; Jesus Will Come By and By,' composed by our foreparents in the dark days of slavery, for even to-day we need such a sentiment to guide us over the rough and rugged road we must travel if we are to reach the sunlight. Now we want to hear from those who have come out to welcome us back, and to rejoice with us in the generous gift of two hundred eighteen acres of splendid farm land given by Dr. D. J. Harris and Mr. N. W. Harris; this is the most heartening prosperity that has yet come to us."

Then different ones of our friends spoke. We can give only the keynotes. Said Rease Berry: "Well, sir, us colored folks been starting up projects of one kind or another ever since de war, schools, cotton gins, and I don't know what all, but we'd always fall out and bust it up 'cause eve'y feller wanted to be de leader. But this school project jest beats eve'ything." Said Oscar Cox: "I'm glad we's spared to meet in this appointed place again. This year we's got a chance to do a whole lot better than ever before. I wants my chillen, an' dese other chillen, to do a whole lot better an' pay attention an' learn a heap an' obey dese teachers, 'cause Fesser sure has brought in a fine crop of teachers." Said Jems McLaurin: "I have but few thoughts. I remember when these school grounds was just a woods and an old field, but the power of education has changed it. I'm only sorry dat I haven't taken more advantage of it myself, though I have given my children the chance." Then Rhodes Donald, who lives fourteen miles back in the woods from the school, said: "I've been settin' here listenin' to the people of this community speaking up for this school and I am well pleased to know that the community is pleased with it—something we seldom see, at least among our folks; there's always someone to throw a stumbling-block in the way. But I'm glad to stand before you once more in life and say that quite an improvement has come over us colored folks. * * * I want to tell you what my boy done. His grandma gave him nine joints of cane an' told him to plant them an' see what he could do. Well, the first year he got seven stalks of cane and saved the eyes and kept on planting an' selling until he's been able to buy him a yoke of oxen from those nine joints. I hope I can get him in with you all and that this school will keep on going up." Mrs. Taylor, the wife of Uncle Ed Taylor, who gave the first forty acres of land, then asked to be permitted to say a few words. Among other things she said: "I have been praying for the school all the time, and I want Mr. Jones to know that he has a real helper in Mrs. Jones; she has just conducted things this summer as they were never carried out before" Then Mrs. Janie Barber said: "I am too full to say much, but I just wanted to let you know I'm praying for you all, and I prays

SOUTHERN WHITE FRIENDS

(Top) Hon. George R. James, on the spot where Goodwill Hall

for that good white woman who gave that printing-press, and for Uncle Asa Turner, and for all of those who have done so much to help." Then Please Williams, a great giant of a man with a laugh that is infectious, brought his typical humor as well as his appreciation into the meeting. Said he: "Excuse me, but I'm jest too full to spress myself. Many times I have got on my knees and talked to God about helping this place to go on. Say, I jest can't say anything; I'm too full. Others have fixed it up an' if I go on in my ignorant way you will forget all o' the good things they have said. I'm goin' to let well enough alone; it's too good a work to fool with." Mrs. Magee followed, saying: "I just want to testify, but like the brother who just spoke I'm so full I hardly know what to say. I appreciate the good works that are going on here. It was five years ago I first heard of this school. I was living way back in the country, forty or fifty miles from here, and one of the teachers came by and told me of it. Well, I didn't see how we could ever get to it as we are poor and have a large family, but I went down the knee way, trusted God, prayed He would help me to obtain the blessing of a school for my children; and now, praise the Lord, we are right in the neighborhood of it. That's why I trust in God. I want to tell you God must be in this place; His works are revealed. My! but I'm happy; the Lord has provided a way for my children. I want you all to pray for me and send me messages of hope." So sincere was this good woman in her appreciation of the school and her trust in the Lord that one aged woman whose early days had been spent in slavery talked and sang and shouted as if she had been at a revival, and others were visibly affected. I then announced that the school had a chaplain for the year who would preach every Sunday morning at eleven o'clock; but before we could introduce him Mrs. Taylor arose and said: "Please excuse me, Professor, but I'm aroused. You have done my heart good. The Lord has answered my prayers. The nearest church being only once a month, I've had to go so far every Sunday to hear the word of the Lord that I have prayed for a better opportunity. The Lord being my helper, I'll be here every Sunday morning."

In the autumn of this fifth year the little school had become so widely known and the responsibility of its management was becoming so much greater each day that it was decided that the time was ripe for applying for a charter. One was accordingly drawn up and submitted to the Attorney-General of the State of Mississippi. I think that in all the world there has never been a group of braver men than those who were formally behind this effort in our development. Mr. W. P. Mangum, our treasurer and the cashier of the Braxton Bank, is one of the most progressive young white men in the State of Mississippi. Hon. R. F. Everett, who is president of the Braxton Bank, is one of the oldest pioneers in the Piney Woods and a veritable patriarch in the country round about. Major R. W. Millsaps, who was in the "Army of the Lost Cause," was one of the foremost men in Mississippi in financial affairs and the most beloved man in the state because of his great philanthropic heart. Captain Asa Turner, well known farmer and pioneer booster, because of his great humanity, loving heart, and Christian association with young men, had become the most beloved man in Iowa. Dr. D. J. Harris, brother of the late well known N. W. Harris, of the Harris Trust and Savings Company of Chicago, is of a family whose business ability, integrity, and helpfulness are known throughout the West. E. N. Taylor, ex-slave, a man of level head and keen business instinct, had become one of the most successful men of the race in Mississippi. Amon Gipson, a staunch man, represents the masses of the people, and Rev. H. L. McClaurin is a farmer and local minister. These

men, together with the principal and his wife, were
those who signed the charter which was submitted
to the Governor of the State, and to whom on May
17, 1913, was formally granted the charter of
" The Piney Woods Country Life School." These
men form the basis of our Trustee Board, and we
also have a special committee for the handling and
investment of any special gifts or endowment.
This committee is composed of Dr. D. J. Harris,
chairman; Mr. W. P. Mangum, and Captain Asa
Turner. Perhaps the most interesting article in
the charter which we acquired is that which reads:
" The cost of education shall, as far as practicable,
be reduced to the lowest point consistent with the
efficient operation of said school and every reasonable effort shall be made to bring education for
country life within the ability of the poorer classes
of the Black Belt."

These were days of rough pioneering, and yet
I love them because of the kindly disposition of
most of the white people in our vicinity, and the
sweet simplicity and devotion of the children of
the soil. And they were dream days as well.
Coming in from the field during the heat of the
day one would sit in the shadows near our quaint
vine-harbored little spring or at evening look across
the moon-washed fields into the great dark woods

Girls in Boarding Department

and dream such dreams as those of which my former teacher, Miss Mary Grove Chawner, wrote from dear Iowa. Said she: "The name *Piney Woods* still appeals to me, as from the first, with the suggestion of beauty in the picture of the tall, straight trees of natural, unhindered, perfect growth. The idea of vigor is there too, in the wholesome, resinous odor, and the wind among the high branches breathing the music of true and good thoughts born above in the sunlight which filters down dimly but gloriously to the listener below. So to me there is the suggestion of poetry and aspiration in *The Piney Woods* which makes it a right name for such a school as yours. Then there is practical suggestion no less appropriate. When the forest is gone to serve its purpose in the world of men, there is the soil, thick-carpeted with pine-needles, the gathered humus of years ready to serve mankind in its way. The name of your paper is no less than an inspiration—*The Pine Torch*—for its instant suggestion of light and its symbolism of the several pieces that must be used together to keep the torch alight."

From the very beginning of the work we had visitors who brought us words of good cheer. After the work had become known beyond our immediate locality we were able to have as speakers and visitors at various times such prominent white men of the South as Major Patrick Henry, Bishop Theodore DuBose Bratton, Rev. G. Gordon Sneade, Hon. B. W. Griffith, president of the First National Bank of Vicksburg; Mr. Thad B. Lampton, vice-president of the Capitol National Bank of Jackson; Col. R. H. Henry, Mr. R. H. Green, Rev. Marcellus Green, Prof. W. S. Bond, State Superintendent of Education; Hon. Bura Hilburn, Mrs. Marjorie C. McGehee, Mr. Bolton Smith, Mr. Frederick Sullens, Hon. George R. James, and we counted among our supporters Mr. W. E. Lampton, Mr. T. J. Thomas, Capt. J. W. Johnson of Pantherburn, Mrs. Grace Jones Stewart, and Dr. J. H. Dillard of the Jeanes and Slater Funds. Within recent years one of our best friends also has been Mrs. Annie M. Malone, of St. Louis, a representative and successful business woman of my own race.

Our first visitor from the North was one frequently mentioned in these pages—one affectionately known everywhere as " Uncle " Asa Turner, but by those who want to be formal as Col. Asa Turner. He came to our first Farmers' Conference, and such an impression did he make that the simple folk of the Piney Woods began to ask immediately after his departure, " Reckon Cap.

Turner ever come back?" or "When is Uncle Asie comin' again?" Then came the late Prof. Laenas G. Weld, formerly head of the Department of Mathematics and later Dean of the College of Liberal Arts of the State University of Iowa, and afterwards president and builder of the three million dollar technical school provided for in the will of the late George Mortimer Pullman. He it was who delivered the dedication address of the dormitory which we called Braxton Hall. In writing of his visit in the university *Alumnus* he said: "There are at the Piney Woods Institute no shops or laboratories or other equipment that are not, from the standpoint of the university man, pitiably inadequate; but there is a definiteness and a strength of purpose, and adaptation of simple means to practical ends, an enthusiasm on the part of pupils and teachers, and certainty of reasonable success in their work, which even the most favored of our colleges and technical schools could afford to sacrifice much to secure." We were also favored in this period by a visit from Rev. Ernest C. Smith, of Chicago. He spent several days with us looking over the plant and meeting the white citizens of Braxton. In recording his impressions he said: "The work is inspired by a high ideal, but is intensely practical and broadly sane. It not

only fits teachers for rural schools and gives industrial training; it is also a center of extension work,
carrying the gospel of better farming, better living, and better schools and churches, throughout a
wide area." Among other visitors were Mr. Roger
F. Etz, of Boston, Mass., and Rev. J. B. Lehman,
a splendid Christian gentleman who has labored
faithfully for twenty-five years at the head of a
school maintained for my people by the Christian
Church. He met the citizens of Braxton and made
a careful study of the community and the school,
and later said: "The people were hungry for the
truth and it was a delight to speak to them the
great truths of God's word, which are the way to
all human progress." Dr. G. S. Dickerman, who
has been interested in Negro education for many
years, and who has traveled extensively in the interest of the Slater Fund for Negro Schools, wrote
concerning our work as follows: "I had never
heard of the Piney Woods country as offering unusual attractions for a colored school. It was sup-
posed to be a sort of white man's country, but
actually in the two counties for which this school
was started the colored children were nearly as
numerous as the white. Certainly the founder
made no mistake in breaking into the Piney Woods
country, for he found a large number of neglected

people eager to welcome him to his undertaking and a great many white neighbors ready to join in the welcome and to assist his efforts." In November, 1913, another friend whose business was entirely different from' that of these other friends, came by to see us. In writing of the school to his home paper, *The Evanston News-Index,* Dr. D. J. Harris said: " Not a little in the way of extension work is being done in the surrounding country, and already the results are apparent in more diversified farming, better tillage, and more tidy homes. Everything is severely plain, not to say crude, but the great Abraham Lincoln acquired much of his training by the light of pine knots in a log cabin, and I know of no work where a dollar will go farther in effecting an uplift of a people, white and black, than in this work that is being done at the Piney Woods School." Other friends who came in these early years were Mr. and Mrs. W. O. Finkbine, Miss Dorothy Finkbine, Miss Charlotte Fleming, Miss Beulah Pack of New Jersey, Mr. and Mrs. E. H. Sunderland of Minnesota, Mr. and Mrs. Arthur Cox, Mrs. Dixie C. Gebhardt, a prominent D. A. R., and Mr. W. C. Harbach. A little later we had the honor of a visit from Hon. James B. Weaver, Rev. Edmund March Vittum, Hon. J. Q. McPherrin, Dr. James Madison Stifler,

Mr. and Mrs. Horace Hollingsworth, Attorney Charles Grilk, Mr. and Mrs. C. P. DeLaittre of Minnesota and Mr. Harold T. Pulsifer, one of the editors of the *Outlook*.

Mr. Abraham Slimmer was the first to begin provision for a permanent income for Piney Woods. He provided a foundation of $2,000 for our endowment in his will.   One thousand was added a little later by Mr. John Oleson of Two Harbors, Minnesota.   More recently Mr. and Mrs. James Gooden of Iowa have made a departure from legacies in giving us $500, expressing the sentiment that they wanted to see this money at work for Piney Woods while they were living.   Mr. Cliff Musser has helped wonderfully by his generosity in providing sums large enough to cover a specific need. Others who have not visited us have put their faith into our venture and helped us in a large way: Mr. Melvin Ellis, Mr. Lafe Collins and Mr. J. L. Collins, Mrs. Minnie McKerral, Miss Flora Dunlap, Mr. T. A. Potter, and the late Mr. George S. Gardiner.

Down in the Piney Woods we had become used to surprises, both great and small, pleasant and otherwise; but when the news came that Mrs. Nellie F. Brooks was coming to help on our teaching force and that, too, free of charge, it was almost more than we could grasp.   It was not so much the great kindness or nobility of her deed that sur-

SOUTHERN WHITE FRIENDS
(Top) Mr. Thad B. Lampton, President, Capitol National

prised us, for we knew she was noble and kind; but, accustomed as we were to the spirit and the reality of sacrifice, we still found it difficult to realize the breadth of the spirit that could cause one to leave surroundings such as hers and come to make her dwelling, even for a little while, in a place like ours. To be sure, at that time Piney Woods was quite an improvement on what it had been in the first few years. We were now using cooking-stoves in the kitchens instead of camp-fires, and the roofs in the sleeping rooms were in such order that we did not see quite so many stars as formerly; moreover, everybody now had a sleeping place, and *nearly* everybody had *nearly* enough covering for the chill autumn nights, or hopes of it before the real winter set in. Furthermore, we were all getting enough to eat now and not so frequently did we casually "drop in" on our friends in the community about meal time and gracefully, though protestingly, accept the unfailing invitation to "set up" to the table. But how would such comfort and affluence as this impress Mrs. Brooks? All of our teachers had been used to better living than they were getting, but Mrs. Brooks had been used to the best. There was her beautiful home in the city of Waterloo, there was her splendid church and her position there as organist, also the Sunday

School in which she had been a teacher for more than twenty years; there were her friends and associates and all the pleasant influences that belong to a life and position such as hers; and Piney Woods had nothing to offer in the way of reward. But Mrs. Brooks was a D. A. R., a Past Regent of the Mary Melrose Chapter, and so with the undaunted spirit of valor and sacrifice that was her heritage she put on the armor and came to Piney Woods to help us fight the good fight of faith. In deep thankfulness we made ready for her coming. Everybody planned, suggested, worked. Hospitality was in the air. Everything was gone over, brushed, scrubbed, and shined. New coats of whitewash were put on here and there; lawns were trimmed; walks were freshly spread with sandy gravel from the shallows of the creek bed. Meanwhile the " Brooks Addition " was going up. This structure, built of fragrant logs from the near-by forest, and boards, some of which were " rived " on the place, was to be the new teacher's home. It was built with all the care we were able to bestow upon it, and when it was finished we hoped that at least as a snug little shelter in the Piney Woods it would do. Inside it was neat and trim and spotless; outside the walls were beyond reproach in their two velvety coats of whitewash. Then **Mrs.**

Brooks came, and was delighted. She took possession of the humble dwelling very much as I
imagine a queen would take possession of a throne,
and with the magic that was hers she soon trans-
formed it into a home. How she accomplished it
I know not. She did not bring much luggage with
her—just a trunk and a few medium-sized, ordi-
nary-looking boxes; but it seemed that into them
she had packed all the essentials for a dainty
and appealing little home. Bits of drapery, gay
chintzes and cretonnes, a bright cushion or two,
filmy lace curtains at the windows, a painting and
etching here and there, a few books, a shining tea-
kettle, a brass lamp with a shade like a big silken
rose, a pair of andirons, two or three little statu-
ettes and groups in marble or bronze, some delicate
china cups and saucers, some teaspoons that rang
like deep-toned little bells, a rug or two that sof-
tened the footsteps like thick woodland—it all made
a veritable wonder-house; and the children there-
about, crude little beauty-worshippers that they
were, fought and schemed for the privilege of working there, whether to wash dishes, run errands, or
sweep the yard. They were simply fascinated by
the place and its owner; and they brought her ferns
and flowers, they, too, began to tidy up with their
small abilities, and they, too, took on many little

ways of politeness and neatness. One mother said that her little boy was "might nigh" ten years old, and the first time he was ever known to volunteer to wash his face was one day when he was going to work for "Mis' Brooks." And from day to day this valiant worker presided over all like a high priestess. She could not express her enjoyment; everything delighted and interested her, from the fat brown little children to the knotty problems of school finances and management. She loved the birds, the air, the flowers, and the big pine woods filling the winds with their resinous fragrance; she loved the duties that confronted her from day to day, and she fairly radiated interest and enthusiasm.

Then one night it rained, dismally, coldly, and long. We heard it, my wife and I, but our roofs being generally rainproof after many patchings we thought little about it, and we thought that all were comfortable for the night. The next morning, however, Mrs. Brooks told us how she had been awakened by a little stream of icy water falling on her face, and how after a while the roof was leaking everywhere and the water settling over the floor in little pools. She joked about it all the next day, and we tried to be a little comical too, but in our hearts we were very sorry.

Brave, noble Mrs. Brooks! The two years that she spent in the Piney Woods will always be remembered by those who were there then; and their influence will be known and felt for generations to come, for as one small seed sometimes produces a mighty tree, that in turn produces thousands of seeds and other trees, just so a noble deed produces other conditions and influences that in turn go widening on and on until they reach eternity.

Miss Doris James is another member of the white race who since the time of Mrs. Brooks has come to share her light with those not so favored as herself. In the office she is doing much that we had not been able to do ourselves. Always cheerful, when our means have been exhausted she has braved the ice and snow of winter to tell our friends in the North personally of our urgent needs. Assisting her at the school is Miss Mable Watson, another member of her race and a most faithful worker.

While these friends and workers were coming to us, I myself continued my efforts for the school by trips to the North, especially in the summer. I had various experiences in seeking lodging in some of the towns in Iowa and Minnesota. Sometimes I slept in depots, once I stayed over night in a box-car, and after one particularly trying experience with two young policemen, a kindly night captain in a police station permitted me to stay until morning on a bunk in a cell. On one occasion, however, I met Mr. Abraham Slimmer, a member of the Jewish race and one of the eminent philanthropists of Iowa. When he found that I had had difficulty in getting lodging, he offered me a place in his home. To-day among the most enthusiastic friends and loyal supporters of Piney Woods are such people of his race as Mrs. Babette Frankel, Mr. J. L. Sheuerman, Mr. Nate Frankel, and Mr. M. Mendelsohn. Among other friends whose practical Christianity strengthened us was Mr. Merrit Greene, a descendant of Nathaniel Greene of Revolutionary fame. At a critical period in our development I received an invitation to speak at several meetings in Marshalltown that Mr. and Mrs. Greene had arranged for us. Mrs. Jones was to give some readings and I was to tell of the school. Never before had the opportunity to meet so many of the best people in one place come to us. We spoke at the First Congregational Church, the High School, a Public School Mothers' Club, the colored Baptist Church, before the veterans of the Soldiers' Home, and especially at a joint session of two chapters of the Daughters of the American Revolution in the colonial living-room of "Edgeworth," the beautiful home of Mr. and Mrs. Greene.

One of the greatest blessings we have ever received came when Mr. W. O. Finkbine and his brother, Mr. E. C. Finkbine, of Des Moines, turned over to us more than eight hundred acres of their cut-over timber holdings which adjoined our school land. This most desirable gift not only gave us assurance of plenty of space in which to enlarge but also provided our supply of fuel, to say nothing of the lumber that can be had when our saw-mill dreams become a reality. Parts of this land are level and can be cleared and farmed, while the steep slopes of other portions will for years to come yield their harvest of stove-wood.

Among the friends who have helped us with their pens are Mr. and Mrs. Paul Lee Ellerbe, two successful writers who in the course of their work have secured for our school splendid publicity in *Collier's, McClure's,* and other periodicals. We first met these friends on the Redpath-Vawter Chautauqua circuit, when we were thrown with them and the Williams Singers, an excellent group of colored musicians, on the third day of the program. At first they had the extreme Southern viewpoint with reference to ourselves and our work, but later a visit of a week to our struggling institution proved to them its merits and they went home to bend their energies toward its up-building.

Perhaps more shadowy tales do not at first seem to belong with " Messages of Hope," and yet it is a fact that each misfortune has only served to strengthen our faith in our friends and in God. One morning just after breakfast we looked up and saw our large school barn in flames. The building was not only a barn but the home of some of the larger boys, who found quarters in the loft. Some years later, on a cold Saturday night, Harris Hall, the dormitory that accommodated more than fifty boys, went up in smoke; this was our best building at the time, and in the fire some of our teachers lost all their possessions. Another blow came with the cyclone that totally destroyed the town of Braxton, three miles from the school. Braxton was our business and banking center, and because the people of the town were so much worse off than ourselves, not only did we have to stand considerable loss on account of the destruction of the bank, but it was absolutely necessary for us to render all the practical aid we could at a time when ordinarily our boys would have been planting our crops for the year. Not a year has passed without some crisis in which only faith could point the way.

Harris Hall, Dormitory that Burned
Boys Living in Tents Afterwards

Each year the increasing needs of the school make $25,000 an absolute necessity, yet again and again we have faced the future without any definite promise of a penny of this amount.

In the South, as may be imagined, I had various experiences, and some are written upon my mind in letters of flame. Of them all I feel that I must tell the story of one, not only because it was the most fearful of all, but also because it reveals the gleam of hope that sometimes lurks beneath the surface even with those whom we consider hostile. Just before we entered the World War a friend of mine who was a minister in a state west of the Mississippi asked me to come and help him in a revival, saying that while I was not a preacher he thought that I might still be able to help him. On the third night I happened to use various words and phrases drawn from military life and operations, telling the people that life itself was a battle, that we must stay on the firing-line, and battle against ignorance, superstition, poverty, and all the evil elements of earth and air. Some white boys who happened to be riding near the church stopped and listened a few minutes and then hastened away to their settlements spreading the news that I was urging the Negroes to "rise up and fight the white people." The next day about noon half a hundred men rode up to the church door and called for me. The people in the church with blanched faces looked toward me, and fear such as I never before saw on human faces looked piteously out of their eyes. I went to the door and said to the men, " I guess I'm the one you're looking for." The leader in a harsh voice ordered me to get in the center. The others closed around me; one threw a rope over my head and drew the noose, and down the road we went. The rest is a nightmare through which somehow sing strains of old Negro melodies. We went to a place rather free from trees, save one with a stout, jagged branch reaching out from it. Under this branch had been piled wood, branches, and fagots, and around the pile was a sea of stern faces, while riders on horses and mules kept coming in an unending stream. A horrible yell rent the air and two or three young boys climbed the tree ready to catch the rope. I was picked up bodily and thrown on the top of the pile of wood, while another roar of noise went up from every throat. Meanwhile I could hear the cocking and priming of guns and revolvers, and from various parts of the crowd random shots had begun to be fired. Then a strange thing happened. One man jumped to the side of the log heap and, waving his hat for silence, demanded that I make a

speech.   With a prayer for help I did speak; I
spoke as I had never spoken before about the life
in our Southland and of what we should all do to
make it better.   I told stories that made the crowd
laugh, I explained what I had really said the night
before, I referred to different white men in the
South with whom I had had helpful dealing, nam-
ing such men as Hon. R. F. Everett, Major Patrick
Henry, Hon. W. P. Mangum, and Major R. W.
Milsaps, and I finally said that I knew there was
no man standing there who wanted to go to God
with the blood of an innocent man on his hands.
Then an aged man wearing a Confederate button
pushed his way through the crowd and waving his
hand for silence, said, "I know those men, they're
all right folks; this must be a good darky."   Turning, he grasped my hand—"Come on down, boy,"
he said, as he pulled me to him and took the rope
from around my neck, then others reached out and
shook hands with me.   God had delivered.   Some
on the edge of the crowd were muttering, for they
felt they had been cheated out of their fun, but
the majority seemed to be with me.   Then someone shouted, "Let's take up a collection for the
Parson;" and several began passing hats.   Some
actually threw money at me.   Some asked, "When
are you going to preach again, Parson?   We want
to be there."   The collection finally amounted to
fifty dollars.

Then one man let me have the use of his horse, he took another, and together we rode back to the church.

As we drew near the church it seemed deserted, but as we approached the door we could hear a mellow voice in prayer. We learned that in their fright the people had scattered to their homes, all save half a dozen of the older men, who had been down on their knees all the time I had been gone asking God to perform a miracle as He did with Daniel in the lions' den and with the three Hebrew children in the fiery furnace. But although they had been praying for my return they could hardly believe it and as they looked at me were frightened enough to run. Then my companion said, " This ain't no ghost; it's the same teacher we took away. It's all a mistake and he's all right; I mean to come out and hear him myself. He's done us more good to-day than he's done you all ever since he's been here. Next time you have a meeting I'll be out and tell you about it." Then he departed, leaving me with my own; and those dear old men, bent with years of toil and struggle, always longing and hoping for the better day that never came, hugged me and cried and sang and prayed, and as we came out of the church the west was aglow with a wonderful sunset, the most wonderful I had ever seen. The stillness was enchanting, and far across the pine trees the fading light brought a feeling of relief and contentment.

After the evening meal was over we sat in a circle, father, mother, grandfather, children, and a few neighbors, and with eager faces they listened to the story as I told it. Then I went to my rest, and in my dreams I seemed to be standing on a huge pile of fagots with the red flames licking the air about me. Then I thought of our struggle in the Piney Woods, of the battle from day to day, of the new strides forward, of the " inching along " to higher ideals and nobler living. I also remembered the softening of the hearts of the men in that terrible crowd and the strange turn of events in a situation that seemed utterly hopeless; and in the largest possible way I had hope not only for my own people, but also for the Southern white people with whom we live.

I saw clearly that that which nearly cost me my life was the identical thing which is the root of most of the racial difficulties—it is misunderstanding. It is this misunderstanding which up to this time has kept back the wholesome realization of existing conditions, which is so necessary to the humane adjustment of the problem, and the breach has widened.

But I am happy to say that there are now more than a dozen different agencies in Mississippi working toward a sane adjustment, all of which makes me feel that there is a brighter day ahead. Moreover, I am confirmed in this feeling by a great sheaf of letters from white men in Mississippi—men who have been in contact with the Negro ever since they were born, who have grown to manhood on the plantations and farms, who have supervised the Negro's work and weighed his cotton and sold it for him. The letters are from every part of the state, but most of them are from the rural districts where the masses of the Negroes live. Some are from bankers, and if there is any man in the world who is capable of judging his fellow-men it is the banker, and all the more able is he when he grows up among the people he is judging. The kindly sentiments of these men tell us that after all we have more friends among the Southern white people than we dreamed of, and the number is growing rapidly. And that is why we are willing to stay here in spite of everything and sing in our hearts:

> "Let me but do my work from day to day,
>   In field or forest, at the desk or loom,
>   In roaring marketplace or tranquil room;
>   Let me but find it in my heart to say,
>   When vagrant wishes beckon me astray,
>   'This is my work—my blessing, not my doom;
>   Of all who live, I am the one by whom
>   This work can best be done, in the right way.'
>   Then shall I see it not too great or small
>   To suit my spirit and to prove my powers;
>   Then shall I cheerful greet the laboring hours,
>   And cheerful turn, when the long shadows fall
>   At eventide, to play and love and rest,
>   Because I know for me my work is best."

VI

WIDENING INFLUENCES

IN the course of the struggle to establish our school in the Piney Woods two matters of the utmost importance to the Negro were being recorded in the history of the state. In 1909 occurred the death of Bishop Charles B. Galloway of the Methodist Episcopal Church, South, one of the most saintly and broad-minded men the commonwealth ever produced, one of those whose eloquence has thrilled thousands of people throughout the world, but whose sense of honor and love of justice were of peculiar interest to the Negro, for whom he was ever ready to take up his pen or raise his voice. It meant a great deal to a struggling race to have a man of such eminence not afraid to stand forth and say: " I have studied, with no small degree of pains, the records of the graduates of most of the leading colored institutions of learning in this country, and I am gratified with the result. I have been unable to find a single graduate from any representative Christian institution that has been convicted of any infamous crime. Education elevates all people, and I deny with all the emphasis of my being the charge that education does not elevate and make better the black man."

The other matter was the heated senatorial campaign of ex-Governor James K. Vardaman. Already while governor of the state this official had abolished the only Negro normal school for the training of public school teachers; and while the *Jackson Daily News,* the organ of the more conservative white people, waged an unyielding fight against him, he went to the United States Senate by a large majority. This critical era naturally affected Piney Woods as it did all other Negro schools, but as the darkest hour always seems to be just before the dawn, it is pleasant to record that ever since then we have had governors who have not used the Negro as campaign thunder and that conditions have seemed to grow better.

The total population of Mississippi is 1,797,114. Of this number 1,009,487, or 56.2 per cent, are Negroes; 95,357 of this number are classed as urban while 914,130, or 90 per cent, live in the rural districts. The percentage of illiteracy among Negroes is 35.6 per cent, which is fairly good, if we remember that nearly 100 per cent were illiterate fifty years ago and that the school facilities which obtain to-day are altogether inadequate. As regards the physical characteristics of the state, there are many people, especially in the North, who think of all the land as swampy. Only the northwestern section, known as the Delta region, is so, and because of the inundation of the Mississippi and its tributaries, this contains the richest soil in the United States. The northeast quarter of the state is the prairie section, a great grain-growing region that fed the Confederacy in the Civil War. The southern half of the state is known as the hill section, and it is here in Rankin county, near the line of Simpson, that the Piney Woods Country Life School is located. One of the inspiring movements in South Mississippi has been the building of the Gulf and Ship Island Railway and the development of Gulfport as a winter resort and a deep-water harbor by the late Captain J. T. Jones, which enterprise is now being carried forward by his daughter and son-in-law, Mr. and Mrs. W. T. Stewart. The success of this tremendous undertaking inspires other enterprises to push forward and the future of South Mississippi grows brighter day by day.

Our county of Rankin contains 791 square miles and Simpson 575. The Piney Woods School, being located near the line, serves both counties as the only graded industrial high school. In a total population of 23,944, Rankin county has 14,294 Negroes; Simpson has 5,969 Negroes, and Scott and Smith, that adjoin Rankin on the east, contain 9,795 more. Thus we have in our immediate vicinity over 30,000 people, more than 50 per cent of whom are illiterate. It should be remembered that this is an entirely rural section of the state, there being only two towns of any size, Hattiesburg, and Laurel, called the Magic City of the state. The wideawake spirit of Laurel is due to the energy and fine spirit of Mr. George S. Gardiner, who pioneered in their mammoth enterprises, and Mr. S. W. Gardiner, his brother. This spirit and accomplishment is being carried forward now by the next generation of keen business men, Mr. P. S. Gardiner, Mr. Arthur Cox, Mr. Charles Green, Mr. Frank Wisner, and Mr. W. B. Rogers. The dense ignorance and superstition of the rural Negroes is due to the lack of effective educational facilities. For over a million Negroes the state furnishes but one Agricultural College, and within the last year this received an appropriation of only $63,000.

It is not to be wondered at, then, that all of the workers at Piney Woods find abundant opportunity for service beyond the immediate bounds of the

Young America
Class Making Baskets of Pine Straw

school. Writing letters, reading letters from sons who have "gone off on the railroad," explaining passages of Scripture, settling family quarrels, acting as judge in neighborhood quarrels, occasionally copying some document for the white people who live near us—these, with the raising of twenty-five thousand dollars a year to carry on the work, are some of my own duties. Once far off in the woods I happened upon a funeral. No preacher being near, the people were preparing to lower the corpse in a rough pine box into the grave without any service when I got off my horse and read some passages of Scripture. At another time a young white man attempted to save the life of an aged colored woman who was trying to cross some railroad tracks before an incoming passenger train. After reading of the deed and making careful inquiry at Jackson, where it happened, we wrote to the Carnegie Hero Fund Commission and are glad to say that the young man received a reward.

During one of our state fairs Piney Woods had on exhibit a large display of live stock. One morning I had donned my overalls and was down helping the boys with the feeding when I received a summons from Hon. Calvin Wells to come to the court house as a witness before the Farm Loan Board, which was traveling about looking up locations for the Farm Loan Banks. I tried my best to impress the members of the board with the advisability of locating a bank in Mississippi; but for the rest of the story it might be best for me to refer to Capt. Frederick Sullens, editor of the *Jackson Daily News,* who wrote in his paper as follows: " One of the most interesting features of the sitting of the Farm Loan Bank Board in this city was the testimony of several prominent Negro leaders, who told of conditions existing among members of their race and the efforts being made by the Negro for agricultural advancement. These Negro leaders made decidedly favorable impressions among members of the board. They obtained a glimpse of the Negro Problem from a new angle, and when they left Jackson many of their former impressions concerning relations between the whites and blacks in the South had been very much revised. A rather amusing incident was the testimony of Laurence C. Jones, principal of the Piney Woods Country Life School, and the impression it made on Herbert Quick, a member of the board. Quick is one of the foremost scholars and writers in America. He resigned a position at $20,000 as one of the editors of the *Saturday Evening Post* to accept a place on the Farm Loan Bank Board, which shows tolerably well what sort of a person he is. When Laurence Jones appeared before the board he commenced quoting Socrates, the first crack out of the box, so to speak. Quick looked at him a bit startled. He was not looking for Socrates from such a source. Jones was telling about the idle Negroes in Mississippi, and quoting the ancient philosopher he remarked, ' Not only is he idle who does nothing, but he is also idle who might be better employed.' Mr. Quick stared at the witness like an entomologist who has discovered some rare bug, but the testimony that came from Jones a few minutes later quickly convinced him that the Negro was not a ' bug ' but a level-headed, progressive, and wide-awake member of his race, who is doing a real and substantial work for the advancement of the Negroes in Mississippi."

In 1916, through the kindness of a friend of Piney Woods, I was given a few weeks' vacation, the first since the founding of the school. Another friend, our own Dr. D. J. Harris, gave Mrs. Jones a trip to Hot Springs to help her recover from a recent siege of illness. I also spent my time at Hot Springs, but was called back to the school before I had been away two weeks. During that time, however, I had delivered several addresses, one being at a mass meeting at the Langston High School. The Hot Springs school board was present and the chairman of the board, Hon. Hamp Williams, a prominent business man and a former member of the state legislature, kindly wrote me a letter of appreciation a few months afterwards.

To us in the Piney Woods the World War brought new responsibilities and obligations just as it did to everyone else. At the very beginning there loomed before me the Officers' Training Camp at Des Moines, to which many of my friends were going. This meant getting into the game early and greater honor; on the other hand there was the family—my wife, mother, two little boys—and then there was the school. Meanwhile I was under a Chautauqua contract to visit some eighty odd towns, and I was also under contract with the State Department of Education for my second term as director of a summer normal school for some three hundred Negro teachers. I turned to my wife and dearest friends for advice, and their conviction was that I should follow out the duties nearest me. When I came to the county seat in the second registration, moreover, and fulfilled the requirements of the Government, my name was officially placed in Class 4A. It was galling to me to think that I was in Class 4, when I had determined that in everything I should be in Class 1; but I resolved that if I could not be in Class 1 on the firing line

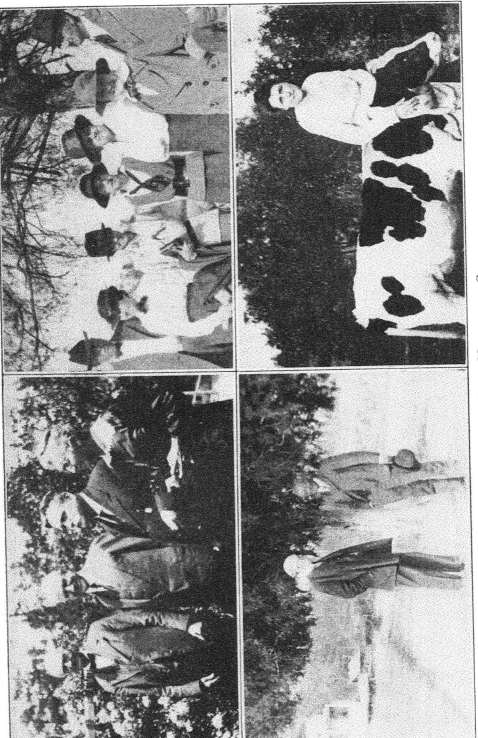

VISITORS FROM FIVE NORTHERN STATES

Mr. W. O. Finkbine an party:

in France I would be in Class 1 on the firing line in America, and so I plunged into war work, and in every address I delivered that summer I put every ounce of energy and enthusiasm. I was State and County speaker for the Liberty Loan Campaign, being engaged in five drives; was chairman of the Colored Red Cross workers in two counties, wherein I conducted two drives; and was speaker in the Thrift Stamp Campaigns; but it was in the First United War Work Drive that I perhaps found my greatest usefulness. In this I was the only member of my race to hold any kind of executive office. Of our boys and the men who were teachers in Piney Woods School more than half a hundred answered the roll-call, and some made the supreme sacrifice for their country. The homes they came from were often the most humble log cabins far away from the main traveled roads, and in them the only books visible were the Bible and perhaps a Sears Roebuck or Montgomery Ward catalogue.

Among the people who live in these homes even yet there is superstition as well as ignorance, and the " conjure man " and the " hoodoo woman " are still to be reckoned with. One day about noon a typical " Uncle Tom " came up just as I was coming out of my garden. Gray dust covered his shoes and clothing, and his eyes moved about with a hunted expression. " Fesser, I'se in trouble," were his first words. I grasped his hand and suggested that we sit down under the old cedar tree. " Why, you knows me," he continued, " sholy you do, Fesser; I's sit an' listened to you speak many a time at Enos Grove Church." " Where do you live?" I asked. " Up here 'twixt Florence an' Plain, 'bout fifteen miles from here." I knew then that something surely troubled him. " Fesser," he continned, " my wife's runned away; dat's my trouble an' I'se come to you 'cause I knows you can help me. Yistidday mornin' I had to go to Jackson, an' Hattie, dat's my wife, said, ' I spec' I's goin' up to Spring Hill to de Missionary dis afternoon.' Well, when I got back dat evenin' 'bout first dark an' walked in an' looked 'round, knowin' she orter been dere, I wondered. I made a little fire in de fireplace an' set down an' rested my head on my hands, tryin' to think. I guess I waited 'bout an hour, yet she hadn't come; then it begin to bother me awful bad. I pushed up de fire an' set till late supper; yit she hadn't come. I neber seed her act dat way before. I jest set dere, didn't know what ter do. I went out to de front gate an' stood with my hands on it 'mos' an hour. Den I went back an' sot by de fire, an' I laid down 'cross de bed, but I couldn't sleep an' I ain't slept none since; an' my heart just kept beatin' and jumpin'. Fesser, dat 'oman never jes' went off; she's been runned off by some dev'lish conjure business. I's been livin' wid her nigh thirty years an' if you ain't never had nary one to do dat way you doesn't know. Look like my heart nigh bust out, jes' jumpin' all de time. You know she didn't jest go off, case she lef' 'bout twenty-five jars of fruit, and her garden done planted, de English peas up dis high, an' she lef' a fine little pig, an' thirty-nine young chickens and twenty-five grown hens in de yard; oh, yes, an' anoder thing, a big trunk in de corner 'bout dat high an' heavy. I don' know what she got in it; I could hardly raise up de corner; she got de key. What you s'pose she done dat for? 'Sides dis, I got a whole lot of ground bedded for corn, an' now it's nobody to plant it. She's a good 'oman; it ain't none o' her doin's at all. It's dis way; a old widow 'oman lived on de place where we is, an' she moved away an' we 'greed to work de place dis year, an' den she'd 'cided to come back, an' case de man what owns de place refused to knock out our 'greement she's mad an' now she's gone an' put a spell on Hattie. Poor Hattie! she jes' don't know whar she is or what she's doin'. Fesser, plenty o' people don' belieh it, but dere's gophers an' conjurers in New O'leans ain't neber been here an' could tell you all you got here, an' dey could tear all your mind up in less 'an a week. De low-down rascals, dey ought to be hung. Some o' dem gits it from de high ones, way back in de far parts o' Virginny; it's called a jack; an' de debils can go to your house while you an' you' wife is sleepin' an' sprinkle some powder on de door step, er plant something dere, an' de nex' mornin' you steps over it an' dey's jest as good as got you as a dollar— * * * No, sir, I ain't hungry a bit; couldn't eat if I had to. I jes' got to keep walkin'. But you can help me, Fesser, you's got de sense; you can work it so dat she'll come back and never leave."

He was very tired, and finally at my repeated urging he sat down to rest, almost immediately falling asleep. The late afternoon shadows were falling across the road when he awoke refreshed and in almost jubilant mood. "I knowed it," he cried, looking at me reverently, "I knowed you could make your han' work if you would. I neher will git through thankin' you, Fesser. I's goin' home an' I knows I'll fin' Hattie dere."

The next Christmas he suddenly appeared with a choice offering from his hog-killing. "You sho deserve dis present," he said, "fer when I got home Hattie was dar, big as life, an' mad as a wet hen case I been out to hunt fer her. She call me a big fool an' ask' me if I was goin' to hunt fer her why didn't I come to de Missionary whar she tol' me she was goin' 'stead o' runnin' askin' 'bout her at ebery do' lak she was some critter strayed off an' lost. Don' you tell her nothin' 'bout my gittin' you ter use yo' han', Fesser, case she'd be madder 'n ever. Women is mighty funny folks, sometimes."

VII

TEN YEARS AFTER

OF the larger buildings at Piney Woods I have told of Braxton Hall, given by the white citizens of Braxton for a girls' dormitory, and Taylor Hall, which is used as a school building, and which also accommodates a few girls. These buildings served well for some years, but as they came in a day when we could build only temporary structures with cheap pine lumber, we kept living on in the hope that they would be replaced by more substantial and enduring buildings. And just as most of the good things which have come to Piney Woods have been unexpected, so we received a happy surprise one day when a young man up in Iowa said, " I will give you $500 in memory of Aunt Lunky, a faithful old mammy who served our family for many years." It was a beautiful thought and a splendid gift. Very soon our boys and even our girls were helping to dig the foundation for a new girls' dormitory, and with the $500 we purchased enough cement to

put down a solid foundation. Then came the war
with curtailment in every department of our work.
One day, however, while looking for Piney Woods
friends in Des Moines with dear Uncle Asa Turner, someone told us that Mr. George W. Dulany,
the young man who had given us the $500, was
captain of Battery F, encamped at the Coliseum.
A successful search through the throng of khaki-
clad soldiers finally brought us to Captain Dulany,
and as he shook hands with Captain Turner,—the
one in the full bloom of strong forward-looking
young manhood, the other with his wise head of
gray telling of the days that had come and gone—
I thought of what a beautiful thing life can be, and
of what a great thing it is to be an American
and to aim to leave the world better than one
found it.

The next time we heard of Battery F it was in
a final training camp in New Mexico, and our
friend was now Major Dulany. After the war
other checks came from him, and finally one for
$3,000, the largest we ever received, to finish the
building, which we dedicated at commencement,
1921, as Dulany Hall. It was our first permanent
building, and within it hangs a picture of Aunt
Lunky, whose serene face has the beauty of truth
and service.

And now as I write this chapter I can see the boys of the school mixing and pouring cement, and I can hear them at work as the walls go upward for our new school building, Goodwill Hall, so-called because of the friends who are giving toward its construction. And there is yet to be built a boys' dormitory to take the place of one lost by fire in 1921, also a domestic science building, a small hospital, a chapel, a boys' industrial building, a girls' industrial building, a dairy barn, a power house, a laundry, and cottages for the married teachers. As all other things have come, some day in God's own time these things also will come.

In the school everything moves by clock and bell. All rise at 5 and breakfast at 6. By 7 everybody must either be at work or in school. At 4 in the afternoon all classroom work is over, and all lights go out at 9.45. Within less than ten years, on hills that were once the abode of stray sheep and rabbits and lizards, there has sprung up a bee-hive of three hundred students, and where there was once but an old log near a cedar tree we have now begun to see buildings of cement and stone. Instead of one cow there are now forty head of cattle, 1,500 acres of land instead of forty, and where there was once but one teacher there are now eighteen faithful workers. I think it was Dr. Charles

Dulany Hall Hon. James B. Weaver o Iowa standing n front

E. Barker, formerly physical adviser to President Taft, who exclaimed as he stood in the midst of the Piney Woods, " What hath God wrought! "

In 1921-22 we enrolled in our boarding department over two hundred boys and girls. These came from thirty-eight counties in Mississippi, and from Florida, Louisiana, and Iowa. To as many more who applied for admission we could only sadly reply that we did not have room for even one more. The boarding students are in two groups. There are those who come to us with all their worldly possessions in a basket or tied up in a red bandana handkerchief, and whose greatest asset is a desire for an education and a willingness to work for it. Such are known as " work students; " they labor through the day and attend school two hours at night. Once on my travels I passed by a large briar patch. I stopped and peered through the thicket, but all I could discern was two large eyes fastened on me. In response to my inquiry the owner of the eyes said, " My name's Willie Buck; I's fo'teen. No sah, I ain't done no kind of work but plow and hoe." In 1922, however, Willie Buck was graduated, and for his commencement part he explained some of the simple and practical uses of electricity, and he spoke in good, clear English. He also knows something of gasoline engine wizardry and has done much of the school's plumbing. " Pa Collins," as he was known by the boys, came and brought his entire family—wife, seven children, father, and mother; all attend school on the credit gained from their work. Another group of students who are able to pay eight or ten dollars a month in cash, work half a day and go to school the other half of the day. All students must be at least twelve years of age to be admitted to the boarding department, but we have even had one who was not sure of his age, but who was more than forty and in the fourth grade. Meanwhile community children from the age of six up to the number of more than a hundred walk daily an average of six or eight miles. One little girl whose mother is dead cooks and sews for five younger children, walks a distance of seven miles, stays through the week with relatives about three miles from the campus, and walks home on Friday evening to put her house in order for the next week.

The following correspondence will reveal something of the class of students who come to us. Here is a letter from one boy who went to France when the call came: " Jackson, Miss., R. F. D. 4, good morning professor, how is all, I is well and all of the family is well. your most welcome letter was received a few days ago glad was I to hear

of the ofer you made. now father were expecting
to help me by selling a cow but the cow eat so
many acorns She died   So father say he can let you
have some molasses if they will be al rite for pay.
if they cont do then i will hafter come and be a
work boy as we aint got no money and i sure
does want to edicate.   Rite me al about it cause
I will work at anything, and the boy that are coming with me are going to let you have a young
heifer for his scholing.   yours truly, Doc Bryant."
A girl by the name of Georgie Lee Myers heard
of the school, and, being without parents and without money, told her friends of her longing for an
education.   For railroad fare and suitable clothing they helped her as follows (and the outline is
given just as she told it to us): Aunt Hester
Robinson gave a pound of butter and a dime,
Grandma Willis a chicken, Aunt Lucy McCornell
" four bits " (fifty cents), Sarah Pernell a chicken,
Effie McCoy a cake and five cents, Sam McCoy
five cents, James Buckner " two bits," Mrs. Church
seven cents, Meal Kyle " two bits," Mollice Pernell
a few things, Chlora Pernell a dime, Bessie Harvey one of her dresses, Washington Lincoln Johnson two pecks of meal, Mandy Willis a dozen eggs.
Concerning this girl her aunt wrote the next fall:
" I am glad to write to you and tell you about the

improvement you has made in Georgia, she is better in the washtub and in the fields and in the kitchen and in the house. She is better everywhere I puts her then she was. She has work so faithful sence she came home I wants to send her back and I wants to pay enough for hir to go to school in the day now if she work in the morning and in the evening after school is out then what will you charge me for hir going to school. Well she says she wants to come if she hafter do like she did last year but I ames to do all I can for her and I wants you and your dear wife to do the same well you write as soon as you get this and let me here so I will no what to do. oh yes there is some boys here who wants to work for their schoolen by so doing git an education by worken a half day and going to school the other half well I am going to send you Georgia's nephew and twoo more I gess they are coming. But you look for Georgia and hir brother first of next month just as soon as you reply to this letter." Georgia did indeed return and we shall hear more of her as one of our graduates.

The academic work of the school is intended to give a good common education and to apply arithmetic, geography, and theoretical agriculture in a practical way. It is our constant endeavor to

Goodwill Hall: The Present School Building, 1922

Constructed wi h s udent labor.   Our girls carried water and bricks, our boys made the brick and erected he building.

teach these boys and girls in the terms of their everyday life, and classes are taken out of doors to the objects measured and studied. We do away with any educational frill and harness the theoretical to the practical life of Mississippi. Arithmetic is applied in determining the cost of making cotton as against the cost of growing corn, in estimating the value of a cow by testing the milk she gives, and in determining the relative value of a Piney Woods " rooter " and a Berkshire. Chemistry is used to show that it has something to do with curing the hams of this Berkshire, with home sanitation, with the preserving of fruits and vegetables, with the making of molasses, and with the testing of seed corn. It is all a training designed to meet conditions as they are and not an effort to force upon the pupil such education as he would need were he to become President of the United States. Some of the students remain to finish only the eighth grade, and then they must end their school days and go out into the world; but they were perhaps already eighteen or nineteen when they came to Piney Woods and entered the third or fourth grade. Some climb upward in spite of the handicap, and for those who have been most fortunate in getting an early start in life our practical teachers' training course in the Normal Department looks forward to a larger life of service.

As for the industrial work, for the boys we have carpentry, blacksmithing, broom-making, shoe mending, printing, and farming; for the girls we have laundering, cooking, housekeeping, sewing, gardening, and poultry raising. Some of the girls also work at shoe mending and broom-making, and every student works for half of each day in some industrial department. Everybody must have at least two years in the agricultural department, and every girl must earn a certificate in the laundry and training kitchen before taking up basketry, and other branches of domestic science and handicraft. Many students stay through the summer in order to earn enough credit to take them through the winter term. In the course of the summer one such girl in order to pay for the following winter's schooling cut brush and small sapling pines, planted corn, dug potatoes, worked in the garden, picked wild blackberries and put them up for the school, set type, washed and ironed, helped in the kitchen at meal times, milked two cows every morning; and when she went home for a few days' vacation she picked cotton, stripped sugar cane, showed her mother the use of wild blackberries learned at school, and also made practical use of her knowledge of sewing. In the industrial and agricultural department as well as in all other departments of

the school there is one ideal we ever hold before
the student body, and that is of the dignity of all
labor. It is best expressed in a motto that I once
saw in the main hall of "Apple Trees," the home
of our friend, Mrs. C. E. Perkins: "Don't forget
that you ennoble your work; it never degrades you.
The only disgraceful thing about toil of any kind
is the half doing of it."

While the school is undenominational the spir-
itual side of the work is not neglected. Indeed the
watchword of the institute is, "Seek ye first the
kingdom of God and his righteousness and all these
things shall be added unto you." The first period
of each morning is devoted to the study of the
Bible. Every Sunday morning at nine our wideawake Sunday School meets. When we can get a
minister it is followed by a preaching service;
otherwise we have an hour of morning prayer. At
one o'clock the Y. M. C. A. and Y. W. C. A. as-
semble, in the afternoon at three comes the Christian Endeavor meeting, and there are evening
chapel services at seven. Every student and teacher
on the campus is to be found at these meetings,
and it is uplifting to see the lines of gray-clad
girls and stalwart young men marching to the different services.

Besides the training in books, industries, and

religion, our students also have a chance to take part in the more spontaneous exercises of clubs and literary societies. The older boys and girls of the school have two agricultural clubs, the Henry Wallace Club and the D. J. Harris Club. These meet on Saturday nights with a program and a joint debate on agricultural topics. The Asa Turner Society is made up of the members of the highest two classes who have for their motto the motto of our Uncle Asa Turner, " To be good, to do good, and to make some money." Then there is the Emily Howland Practical Life Society, made up mainly of girls from the printing and shoe-mending departments. These clubs fulfil a valuable purpose in that they have not only given splendid training to the boys and girls, but also because they give them an opportunity for self-expression.

The teachers who come to us are generally selected with regard to their ability to teach not only books but some industrial subject, so that they are found in the shops or field when not in the schoolroom. Piney Woods will always be grateful for the good work done by Mr. and Mrs. Yancy. Mr. Yancy had been taught carpentry by his father and grandfather, and helped especially in the erection of the first buildings. Mr. Reden was a young man in Iowa whom for two years I urged to come South. He served in our academic department, later married one of our teachers, Miss Mary E. Martin, who also had worked faithfully for a number of years, and now he and his wife are in public school work in Sunflower county, and, by virtue of their experience in Piney Woods, where we instruct teachers and pupils always to do that which will bring about a better understanding between the races, have succeeded in getting the school authorities in their section to do more for public education than they ever did before. Mr. McGilberry, Mrs. W. C. Dixon, and Rev. E. J. Penney and Mrs. Penney are also among those whom we remember with most gratitude. Mr. McGilberry has a natural gift for mechanical work and the spirit of a true missionary. Rev. Mr. Penney was our faithful chaplain for two years, and his instruction in the Bible will never be forgotten. To-day eighteen teachers altogether are laboring faithfully for the upbuilding of the work and the elevation of the surrounding country, and they are working more for the good that they can do than for any financial consideration. In connection with them we remember also the interest of two of our local trustees, Mr. Amon Gipson and Mr. Hector McLaurin. These men have been almost weekly visitors on the campus and have always been at the service of the school night or day, whenever we have called them.

As the years have gone by naturally our field of service has become more extended. All through the year the teachers do extension work in person, sometimes in a single home, again in a neighborhood meeting or in a country church, sometimes simply in an outdoor meeting called for the formation of an improvement club. We found some of the people working on " halves," that is, they gave half of what they made for their provisions during the year; some rented or leased, but in any case their debts at the end of the year covered all that they made. Now the spirit of buying land possesses many; they desire to be independent small farmers, consuming with economy, so that they might get ahead. Many are still living in old log cabins built before the war, but for the most part the homes are whitewashed or painted, and some have even built new houses. In some places glass windows have appeared where there were only wooden shutters before, and in many other ways signs of progress are discernible. Indirectly or directly our workers thus influence for good more than nine thousand people each year.

Each year we hold at the school a Farmers' Conference, and in this meeting experiences are exchanged. We always endeavor to have at these gatherings a good speaker who will inspire the farmers to better living as well as better systems

of working their land. On these occasions such
men as Captain Turner and Prof. P. G. Holden
have met face to face six hundred earnest peasant
folk from two states and nineteen different settlements. During the ten years that these confer-
ences have been meeting more than six thousand
acres of land have been purchased by colored farmers in the vicinity of the school, which is more
than was purchased in the previous twenty years.

Although the school is but ten years old, the
records of our ex-students and graduates are ample
evidence of the good of the work and constitute a
perpetual reward and incentive. It was just four
years ago, in May, 1918, that Piney Woods sent
out from the Normal Department its first class.
Ah, that first class, the class of 1918! How they
worked! How they loved Piney Woods! Of that
class those who are still connected with the school
in one way or another are Charles M. Shed,
who is in charge of the printing office and the assistant treasurer; Miss Eva L. Spell, the school's
accountant; Miss Ella Carter, who worked four
years in a private family in Cedar Falls, Iowa, in
order better to prepare herself to take charge of
our academic and musical departments; and Miss
Pauline Williams, who also attended the Iowa State
Teachers College, has endured many hardships as

financial agent of the school, and is now in charge of the physical training of the girls. Another of our young men, R. D. Otis, we sent to Three Oaks, Michigan, to learn practical methods of farming. He succeeded in building up the dairy business and in graduating after four years from the Three Oaks High School with a little over a thousand dollars in cash and a recommendation from every business man and banker in town. He is now in his second year at the Iowa State Agricultural College. Of the class of 1919, two members were actively engaged in educational work with headquarters at the school for two years—Miss Georgia L. Myers, who as county industrial supervisor for Simpson county had under her charge twenty-three schools and three thousand children, and Miss Gerthie Polk, who as county industrial supervisor for Rankin county had in charge fifty-three schools and five thousand children. Responding to a Macedonian call from Georgia Lee Myers one day, I journeyed back from the main-traveled roads and found her teaching in a little country school and trying to carry out what she had learned at Piney Woods. No one had ever before undertaken such work as hers in the community where she was, and she had to work against opposition and indifferences as well as general inconvenience and poverty.

However, she had taken charge of the little dilapidated school, helped whitewash it inside and outside, had put in two glass windows, built a fence around the yard, and set out some trees. After I had spoken to the people one of the most progressive men of the community came to me and said: " Fesser, we ain't never had no teacher in here like Miss Georgia, an' we wants to keep her all de time; but she says she wants to go back to youall's school, so if we hab to git another one we wants one jest like her." Somewhat more recently, after a year of trouble and trials of every kind, with help from Mr. Julius Rosenwald's Negro Educational Fund, Georgia Lee Myers has succeeded in raising enough money to put up a modern rural school building where she and Miss Nancy Young, of the class of 1921, are now teaching. The splendid work of Miss Gerthie Polk in bringing about a change at the Green Hill School needs little comment. I only wish, however, I could bring home to my readers what it means to raise six or seven hundred dollars among a people who really want the better things of life but whose ignorance and superstition literally sow with stumbling-blocks the path of one who essays to help them better their situation. In the class of 1920 one strong young man, DeWitt Talmage Mason, reversed the usual order of things by going back to the farm while his father went to town to work. His modern ideals of farming and his general knowledge of carpentry and blacksmithing have revolutionized the old farm, and he and his wife, who is also from Piney Woods, command the respect and admiration of both white and colored people.

Miss Estella Otis, of the class of 1920, first took up stenography under the tutelage of Mrs. Brooks. After her graduation a friend of the school helped her to complete the course of her choice at Des Moines College, and she is now busy from day to day sending out the *Pine Torch* and carrying forward the correspondence of the institution. Thus out of a total of thirty-eight graduates, five are still connected with the institution and the others are engaged in teaching, farming, buying homes, attending higher institutions of learning, or following other useful pursuits.

The other day my wife and I went out for one of our occasional tours of inspection. In the industrial shops we found boys at work blacksmithing, one making a pair of hinges for a farm gate, one shoeing an unruly mule, and another filing a wheel. In the carpentry shop two boys were at work, one at the turning lathe, the other repairing

Commencement   1922

a table. Across the road several boys were making brooms out of straw that they had helped to grow, and others were mending shoes. Then we went to the piggery, where we smiled at the thoroughbred hogs that had taken the place of the razor-backs we started with. Several boys were spraying them with creosote dip, while another boy was filling a trough with water piped down from a hillside spring. To our right geese and ducks were diving and paddling in a large pond.

We went over the hill and saw the lambs at play and the wise-looking goats browsing upon the shrubs; and then looked over an experimental patch of alfalfa on the Harris farm, the first grown in these parts. Then we climbed over a five-foot woven wire fence that had taken the place of a rail fence, and, crossing a field of oats, went around by the grist mill, where the boys were grinding into grits and meal for the school's commissary the corn they had raised the previous summer. Here also was the large cane mill, which our friends gave us last summer, and there was the big twelve horsepower gasoline engine sent us by our good friend, Captain Turner. We thought of the first letter he had written: " I like what you are doing in your corner of the vineyard;" and we passed on by some boys with two double-mule teams turning over the earth. Farther on we saw another team at work and a boy planting potatoes and another setting out onions.

At the barn we found several boys hauling out fertilizer, another putting the evening rations in the troughs for the cows and mules, while another was currying Capt. "Jersey Jinks." We passed the poultry plant and saw the Plymouth Rocks and journeyed on over the hill to the laundry where a dozen girls were at work in order that they might "plant their feet on higher ground." We passed the domestic science room and saw the cooks in their neat white aprons and caps, and then came to the printing office where we heard the steady beating of the gasoline engine pulling our new press, made possible by such generous friends as Mr. George A. Joslyn and Mr. Joseph R. Noel. A crippled young man of the class of 1918, who had come to us a few years before, was running off the *Pine Torch,* while several girls were at work folding and addressing and wrapping the papers. We passed on to the girls' industrial shop where we found some girls sewing, others making baskets out of pine straw, some weaving rag carpets, others mending shoes, just as steadily as when Mrs. Jones left them. We went on to the school building and heard the hum of the primary tots, and in the library a Bible class was in session.

We went into the office and looked out of the window toward the barrel room where we keep for distribution to needy students the boxes and barrels of clothing from the North, and we thought of the lives that had been saved for service by such means as these. We looked around in the office at the table upon which this typewriter stands, that is telling the story, a gift from the loving hands of Mrs. Charles E. Perkins, and in the other corner we noted the desk from the home of our early friend, Mrs. James G. Berryhill, at which the little woman writes, often until late in the night. Then we looked at the letter files that contain the hundreds of cheering messages to "strive on" that have come to us like good words from another world and have brought the spray for our human orchard.

I wish I might tell you that Piney Woods is an ideal school, that it holds out to all who would enter the torch of learning and opportunity; but we are still in the throes of those growing years when our boys are quartered in temporary barracks and often in tents, and when our girls, to make room for one more, often sleep four in a bed. Every month in the year we refuse boys and girls who would willingly work for the most meager opportunity of education.

Many of our dreams are yet unfulfilled. To-day, in a shabby half-log hut, our girls do the washing for the two hundred boarding students on boards that are often home-made. No church building has as yet made possible the gathering in of the hundreds of our people about the community for intelligent divine worship on the Sabbath day. No teachers' or faculty living quarters have as yet been provided, and often our splendid workers have been crowded together in a fashion hardly less rough than that of our students, more than one of them sharing the tents and barracks.

Other departments are still limping toward the perfection to which Piney Woods aspires; yet we can but think of the time ten years ago when we had only the desire to serve and when this was an abandoned haunt of the owl and the bat, with only a shelter for wandering sheep. And we think, my wife and I, of our two little boys and of the host of other boys and girls who have come and gone, and we lift up our hearts in thanks to God for the kind friends who have made possible all that we see about us in Piney Woods to-day. Then we ask that we may be spared to see the future lives of the boys and girls as they go out to carry the pine torch of Christian service to the many still in darkness.

For "the desire of our hearts," as Captain Turner puts it, is not to build up a great school as the world considers greatness, but a simple little country life school that will carry the gospel of better farming, better living, better schools and churches, to those who live back from the main-traveled roads. Just to reach this corner of the vineyard, to teach that Christianity is to be used seven days in the week, to show those whom we serve how to make two blades of grass grow where only one grew before, and, above all, to realize and practice *Noblesse Oblige* so that those who receive the blessings will pass them on to the darker corners of the vineyard.

And so our endeavor here in Piney Woods is that the school and those who go out from it will ever make true the message from the sterling-hearted grandmother of Edward Bok: "Make you the world a bit more beautiful and better because you have been in it."

AFTER WORD

THIS account by no means exhausts the story of Piney Woods: No word is said of the splendid business men of Marshalltown who have put their funds together to make big things possible here. One thousand dollars from this source went into Goodwill Hall.

Nor have we paused to give praise to the pastors and many churches who have opened their doors for us to speak and sing; nor to the editors over the states who have printed bits of information and letters and notices without stint. And to the Sunday Schools and other societies who have sent their money, their boxes of clothing, and their books to help us, we owe far more space than we have dared to take in this little book.

To white friends around us who have braved criticism and scorn which came because they were kind enough to associate with us and with our white teachers, even in the face of popular opinion, we are especially grateful, though we have not said so in detail in these pages.

Other things are left out: Serious occurrences have been averted: There is the time when some rowdy white boys thought to come into our rough little chapel and "clean up" the place, when Mr. Homer Barwick, one of our Braxton white friends, heard of it before we did and came up and stood at the door with his shotgun. There is the threat, revealed long afterward, to dynamite our little plant, when the counsel of Mr. William Pattie, another of our good white neighbors, saved us.

Several honors would be worth recording: Piney Woods is the youngest school in the state following the great Tuskegee idea, yet the State Department of Education invited me to be one of the five in the state to work out the accredited courses of study for standardizing the Negro schools. The others were Professor Z. T. Hubert of Jackson College, Professor R. S. Grossley, Assistant State Supervisor of Negro Schools, President W. T. Holmes of Tougaloo, and Professor L. J. Rowan of Alcorn. At another time I was invited to speak for my people before the newly organized State Illiteracy Commission.

Leaders among the colored race who have visited Piney Woods are hardly mentioned: We owe them much, both for the inspiration they have been to us and for the financial help their hearty recommendation has brought to us. Among these are Mr. Louis Gregory of Washington, D. C., William C. Craver, Field Secretary of the Y. M. C. A., Hon. W. T. Vernon, former Register of the Treasury, Professor Rev. William H. Holloway of Talledega, Professor W. B. T. Williams of Hampton and Tuskegee Institutes, Miss Josephine Pinyon and Miss Catherine Lealtad of the Y. W. C. A., L. K. Atwood and Prof. E. H. McKissick, both of Mississippi, and C. J. Halloway, Director of the Extension Department of Tuskegee, who, upon recommendation of the State Department of Education, appointed the writer to serve as the first representative of the Rosenwald Fund for rural schools in this state.

There are other incidents: the graduating of my own mother from the broom-making department of Piney Woods; the cow dispute in which more sympathy was aroused through the ills we had to suffer because our skin was brown, than can ever be recorded.

Very little mention is made in this volume of the vital part Mrs. Jones has had in the school. To record it would make a book itself and then it would be half-told, for it is too great to be fashioned into words. Only the lives of those she has helped can express it.

Printed in United States of America